# NO-FAULT LIVING

Gerald Albert, Ed. D.
WITH Scott Michel

**Impact Publishers**
Post Office Box 1094
San Luis Obispo, California 93406

Library of Congress Cataloging-in-Publication Data

   Albert, Gerald, 1917-
      No-fault living / Gerald Albert with Scott Michel.
         p.      cm.
      Includes index.
      ISBN 0-915166-72-0  (paperback : acid free)
      1. Interpersonal conflict.  2. Faultfinding.  3. Blame.
   I. Michel, Scott.     II. Title.
   BF637.148A42  1991
   158' .2—dc20                                    91-15063
                                                       CIP


Printed in the United States of America on acid-free paper
Published by *Impact* 🐌 *Publishers*
POST OFFICE BOX 1094
SAN LUIS OBISPO, CALIFORNIA 93406

# CONTENTS

*Preface*

1. *The Blame Game* — 1
2. *The No-Fault Alternative* — 5
3. *What Is No-Fault Living?* — 9
4. *"It's Not MY Fault" — and Other Songs of Love* — 13
5. *Toward No-Fault Marriage* — 25
6. *Guilt: The Legacy of Blame* — 35
7. *How Grown Up Are You?* — 43
8. *Unblamed Children and No-Fault Parents* — 47
9. *Fault-Free Friends and Lovers* — 59
10. *How to Succeed in Business Without Really Blaming* — 69
11. *The Golden Age of No-Fault* — 77
12. *Nor Blame Thyself* — 91
13. *Masking, Maneuvering, Manipulating...* — 97
14. *So What Do You Do About It?* — 105
15. *Putting It All Together* — 117
16. *The "Magic 10" Guidelines for Successful No-Fault Living* — 125

*Postscript* — 127
*Post-Postscript* — 129
*Index* — 131

# *DEDICATION*

*To my wife, Norma,*
*the most unselfish person I've known*
*— and the best natural example I've met*
*of the no-blame principles espoused in this book.*
G.A.

# *PREFACE*

$\mathcal{T}$his book offers a rare opportunity — an opportunity to make a major change for the better in your life, without having to pay a major price.

By consciously and deliberately modifying one aspect of the way you relate to other people, you can improve the feelings they have toward you... and, in turn, your feelings toward them.

By doing so, you can increase significantly your prospects for success in almost everything you plan and do.

Read on.

*Abandon Blame, All Ye Who Enter Here*

*1*

## THE BLAME GAME:
## GETTING TO KNOW
## THE PLAYERS

*D*oris and Ben* had returned home after an enjoyable
evening dining out with another couple. They felt
comfortable and warm toward each other, still
responding to the effects of good food and wine. At
bedtime they were particularly affectionate.

But when they awoke Doris slid from the bed sullen
and silent. Recognizing the warning signals of a brewing
tempest, Ben remained prudently silent. He put on his
robe and moved toward the shower.

"Aren't you going to say anything?" she demanded.

Ben stopped and looked at her quizzically. "What do
you want me to say?"

___

*All names of people in this book, except those of public figures, are
fictitious, to protect their identities.

*1*

Ben remembered a line he had read. "Now comes the water routine," he sighed, looking expressively to the heavens.

"Why do you have to be that way?" she complained. "You were too rough again last night. You *hurt me!*"

"I was not too rough!"

"I tried to tell you, but you were drunk."

"That's crap. I had less to drink than you did."

"That doesn't matter," she persisted. "You're too rough even when you haven't been drinking. You're always too rough. You're selfish. You only think about *your* needs!"

"I'll tell you what the problem is," Ben snapped, turning to face his wife directly. "Nothing's good enough for you. You're always complaining. I wasn't too rough at all. That's how I make love, okay? What do you want — a man or a dishrag?" He strode into the bathroom and slammed the door behind him.

Doris glared at the closed door, telling herself he really would have preferred to make love to the other woman in their foursome the night before.

At that moment she hated him.

* * * * * * * *

Home early from work one evening, Pete settled in his chair with the newspaper. Nearby, Lorraine, his wife of 15 years, struggled to fold several sets of heavy curtains she had ironed earlier.

Sighing heavily, she shot glances at Pete which he ignored. Her anger began to build until finally, tired, sweaty and out of breath, she let the partly folded curtains drop to the floor. "What's the matter with you?" she asked sharply. "Can't you see this is too heavy for me? You know how my back is — don't you care at all? Why can't you *ever* show any consideration? Give me a hand here!"

Pete slammed the paper down. He knew she was having a problem, but he was comfortable in the chair, and tired from his own day's work. Now, moved by a combination of guilt and resentment, he stood up and helped her finish the job.

"Just put them there, please," Lorraine said coldly when they were done. Then she left the room without thanking him.

\* \* \* \* \* \* \* \* \*

The unpleasantness that marks these two exchanges is painfully obvious. The problem *appears* to be that the partners had too little consideration for each other, became too easily irritated with each other, and did little to control it.

What is more difficult to see is the fundamental error in the *assumptions* the husbands and wives made about each other. They were operating on a deeply harmful set of basic beliefs about the right and wrong way to act in human relationships. Later we'll look closely at how they *could* have been responding to each other, on the basis of a dramatically different assumption that produces love and caring, rather than resentment and anger.

By understanding the fundamental error involved, and correcting it, relationships of all kinds can be made deeper and more rewarding. That's what this book is all about.

Clients in my practice who have explored the ideas offered here, and incorporated them in their own lives, have seen dramatic improvements. After 30 years as an analytic psychotherapist and marriage counselor, I have seen many relationships crippled by long-held misguided beliefs — *beliefs probably held by most people you know*. And I've seen some wonderful changes when new understandings take their place.

The new understandings outlined in this book could change your life, too.

*2*

# THE NO-FAULT ALTERNATIVE

*D*oes there always have to be someone wrong in every dispute? And someone else right? Isn't it possible that sometimes neither person is right? Or wrong?

No matter how strongly two people differ, it *may* be possible for both to be right; valid, but contrary, points of view can co-exist.

It took many years for widespread acceptance of the "no-fault" concept for auto insurance. Since then, in those states which have no-fault laws, innumerable accidents have occurred, and innumerable settlements have been reached without the need for one driver or another to be "wrong."

Family practice attorneys took almost as long to define guidelines for "no-fault" divorce. They finally recognized that divorce is difficult enough without always forcing one partner or the other to be the "bad" one.

Bitter battles to prove which spouse is the better parent, or the more faithful partner, often have eclipsed the simple need to provide workable separate lives for people handcuffed together in miserable, unholy matrimony (wed*locked*, in truth!).

But auto insurance and divorce merely scratch the surface of no-fault. In recent years it has become clear that the same concept can — and should — be applied to *all* relationships in life.

If the simple logic of "no-fault" becomes an essential part of all your relationships, the onus of blame is removed. And the benefits can be enormous.

Imagine what your life would be like if you'd never been blamed for anything you did. Imagine what it would be like if others had never made you feel guilty in their efforts to control your actions.

What do you think the results would have been if you'd never been saddled with the burden of blame-loaded guilt, but had simply been required to change behaviors that your parents objected to, with a clear explanation of the reasons for their objection, and with reasonable rewards or punishments following directly?

Years of individual and family counseling practice have convinced me that most people, treated this way, will be significantly healthier and happier.

Blaming and fault-finding produce destructive lifetime consequences, in children *and* adults.

\* \* \* \* \* \* \* \* \*

When Max, a 30-year-old assistant editor with a small book publishing firm, came for therapy, he had slept a total of six hours in three nights. He had an opportunity to become an associate editor, but he was so concerned about the new responsibilities that he was lucky he got any sleep.

He had been barely able to develop control of his anxieties about making errors in his present position. Yet he had succeeded, and done well at the job, although at the cost of countless hours of overtime work and nights of lost sleep.

Now, eye-to-eye with the new assignment, his fears had become so crushing that he felt unable to manage them at all, and saw himself on the verge of a breakdown.

The heart of Max's problem turned out to be a childhood and adolescence spent as an only child in a household where the father's training consisted mostly of severe admonitions against error, and even more severe blame for every mistake that occurred. "You have to do it *right*, or I can't accept it," Max was told. Or, "Be sure you remember *exactly* what I told you, or you'll be punished."

And the slightest error would result in: "How can you be so *dumb*? Didn't I tell you what to do?" Or: "How can you be so careless? You'll just never amount to anything when you grow up!" The father, of course had never achieved what he wanted for himself in life. He certainly wanted better for his son. But Max, as a child, had no way of knowing or understanding this.

It was no wonder that Max lived in dread of making even the smallest mistakes. Extended treatment finally helped him work through his problems to a large extent, but it's unlikely he will ever be a really comfortable, self-confident person.

An extreme example? Perhaps. But a great many people do live with similar difficulties.

Your relationships need not suffer from such unnecessary and harmful burdens. No-fault living can be a reality. You can make it so.

But please note: When you give up blaming and faulting, you don't stop expecting people to be responsible for their actions. Nor do you stop seeking to change things for the better, in others and in yourself.

It's just that there are more effective ways than blaming to accomplish this.

P.S. My editors have encouraged me not to include both terms — "blaming" and "faulting" — in describing the destructive behaviors addressed in this book. Nevertheless, I believe it is important to include both. *Blaming* is one kind of destructive action in a relationship; *faulting* (or fault-finding) is another. The first produces guilt or shame. The second causes resentment or lowered self-esteem — or both. This book is about *both* behaviors.

# *3*

## *WHAT IS NO-FAULT LIVING?*

*W*ithout being aware of it, most people live a rather significant lie.

Would you prefer a lifestyle centered on good, warm, lasting relationships, or one that puts the premium on always being "right"? You're pretty sure to answer, "Good relationships — of course." And perhaps think me silly for asking.

But when you get right down to it, most people *live* as if always being right is indeed more important than good relationships. Because of some very powerful needs, especially the need for self-esteem, humans fight like crazy to avoid admitting they're wrong. They use all kinds of evasions, excuses, alibis, rationalizations — even outright lies.

*Self-esteem* is produced in part by *esteem from others*. When I tell you I think you're right, I'm *approving* you — that is, giving you esteem. When I say you're wrong, I'm depriving you of esteem.

The need to use almost any means available to prove one's rightness is largely responsible for many of the failures that plague relationships. Relationship-destroying *blaming* and *faulting* are intrinsic tools of this need to be right.

You learn to impose guilt and shame early in life, by having them imposed on you, or seeing them used on others. They fill the novels and plays in our literature, and we hear stories and sermons illustrating them in our churches and synagogues.

Sigmund Freud considered the capacity to feel guilt and shame to be instinctive. According to Freud, somewhere in the dim past humankind discovered that these feelings could be used to control others. This knowledge was then passed down by example, becoming part of the fabric of our culture, our educational systems and our religious institutions.

Because others are as vulnerable as you are, blaming and faulting usually offer the easiest way to change their behavior. But the price for this is, in fact, prohibitive.

It has come to be considered "natural" to influence others by assessing fault or blame. You may slip with the greatest of ease into such phrases as "You never...," or "You always...," followed by words of fault-finding or guilt-imposition. And it is certainly true that these pressuring expressions often succeed in bringing about a change — however temporary — in behavior. But they also bring some harmful and unwanted *feelings*.

When you blame or find fault, you probably assume that the other person will feel remorse or regret, in addition to changing behavior. This will signal that you have made the point: you are "right" and the other person is "wrong," satisfying your self-rightness need. Now, you assume that everything will be fine. The other person will now behave "properly."

But experience has shown, over and over, that the more likely effects are feelings of resentment, anger, frustration and, in extreme cases, even hatred.

To make matters worse, if the other person's behavior doesn't *stay* changed, you feel deceived and betrayed, and the cycle begins again. Inevitably, blaming and fault-finding end up destructive and self-defeating.

It is important to realize that this does not mean you should overlook behavior that needs to be changed. It simply means you should avoid methods which work more harm than good, which cause feelings of guilt or self-belittlement. To build loving, caring relationships, you have to treat others with acceptance and respect — not blame and fault-finding.

The logic of breaking the cycle is evident. Doing so can make life vastly more satisfying for yourself and for those around you. When you pattern your life to actively *avoid* blaming others, you actively avoid pushing them away — and you permit closeness to grow, instead.

No-Fault Living is not a panacea. It doesn't simplify and resolve all the complexities of life. But it does offer a way to make dealing with them more successful, more rewarding and more fulfilling.

The rest of this book deals with the nitty-gritty of accomplishing that.

The next chapter presents examples of the damage these traditionally accepted behaviors can do to even the most promising marital partnerships. Then we move on to look at the sources of this damaging lifestyle, in childhood and adolescence, and the harm it can do in other phases of your life (parenting, friendships, romance, career and aging). Finally, we explore a common sense method of modifying your lifestyle to take care of these problems for the benefit of everyone — most especially you.

# 4

## "IT'S NOT MY FAULT" — AND OTHER SONGS OF LOVE

"*W*hy *shouldn't* I blame Harry if he does something to hurt me?" asked Tricia, sitting long-legged and blonde on the couch in my office. Her husband leaned forward resentfully in the chair he had deliberately moved to a position several feet away from her.

"Does it make things better when you blame him?" I inquired.

"No, not usually. But I *feel* it should. Why can't he change? Why doesn't he see that what he's doing is *wrong*?"

Harry started to respond, then clamped his lips together. His mask-tight expression spoke volumes — resentment, frustration, rage.

That brief moment said it all.

### *Happily Ever After?*

Most couples march to the altar with dreams of a blissful future together. For an appallingly large number, the dream turns out to be a fairy tale more grim than Grimm.

Most people are taught at an early age that marriage is an eminently worthwhile life goal. The play time of many children is often devoted to "playing house," as Mommy or Daddy. The passions of our adolescence are often focused toward it. Our religions hold it as a sacred union.

Despite mixed reviews in recent years, most young people still expect to take the nuptial vows some day.

"Living together" has its charms for some, especially since it isn't burdened with social and legal impediments to easy separation. But its inherent lack of commitment and permanence deprives it of the *security* aspects unique to marriage (when marriage works).

When it does work, marriage offers the partners an opportunity for special intimacy, long-lasting feelings of security, and encouragement of personal growth found in no other relationship. Married people live longer and remain healthier, as a matter of statistical fact.

But the social and personal pressures favoring marriage fail to prepare people for the reality that, besides being the ultimate relationship, it is also the most difficult.

Studies indicate that a large percentage of marriages end in divorce. In fact, there are about half as many divorces as new marriages each year. Although the exact figures are disputed, they are formidable.

In the close quarters of married life, all the ordinary problems of relationships become mercilessly intensified. In the context of the boiling cauldron of marital problems regularly brought to the counselor's office, it sometimes seems surprising that the divorce figures aren't even higher.

How often have you seen personal qualities that worked beautifully in a friend's single life falter dismally in matrimony? How often have you known someone who enjoyed smooth relationships at home with parents, sisters and brothers to suffer a rocky relationship with husband or wife? So often a man or woman in business, expert at managing people of all kinds, can't seem to "manage" a relationship with *one* person at home.

No-Fault Living offers an explanation — and significant help — for many of these problems.

\* \* \* \* \* \* \* \* \*

Selma and Joseph had been married five years. Both worked in middle management, she in a college personnel office, he as an assistant sales manager for a stationery supplies distributor.

Selma had learned, during childhood and adolescence, that she could control many situations by resorting to feminine "wiles," and appealing to the generosity of others. This worked for her because she was attractive and engaging, and gave the impression of trying to please.

Joseph had a *mother* who was similarly soft and feminine — but was very strong, in subtle ways. His father, on the other hand, always left it to his wife to be the take-charge person in the family.

With his parents as his model, Joseph grew up expecting equally capable management skills from a wife, even one as softly feminine as Selma. She expected her husband to take over and care for her, as everyone else in her life had seemed to do.

Neither Selma nor Joseph lived up to the other's expectations. He waited for her to make decisions and give direction to the relationship. She waited for him to do the same. Both were continually disappointed and frustrated. Each automatically *blamed* the other.

After many rounds of complaining and sulking, they finally turned to marital therapy for help. By this time a tremendous amount of resentment and frustration had built in each of them.

Selma's fervent complaint was: "He never takes charge, the way a man should!" After which she added sadly, "I can never depend on him when I need him."

"Why does she expect me to take care of *everything*?" was Joseph's retort. "She's so...useless!"

In the counseling situation, fortunately, such accusations can be focused on and their motivations explored. Adjustments and adaptations can be made. Accusations such as "useless" and "irresponsible," which are bound to result in hurt feelings, retaliation and/or withdrawal, can be spotlighted.

Sometimes, a seemingly-more-satisfactory-but-infinitely-more-destructive kind of compliance may take place on the surface but will be coupled with a festering resentment at deeper inner levels.

With so many marriages floundering, there is an urgent need for improvement in the way we conduct our marriage relationships. Such a change does not necessarily involve probing sessions with a therapist. Not all troubled marriages are best helped in this way. Indeed, it is highly unlikely that most couples are oriented toward professional help when the frictions begin. Many people in need of counseling help are deterred for financial, religious or cultural reasons.

But most couples *can* be taught to make a single, critical alteration, and pull most of the poisonous sting out of their demands for "reform" in each other's behavior, while encouraging constructive and nurturant adjustments at the same time.

### *Most Couples Can Learn Not to Blame*

Blaming and fault-finding are *learned* ways of influencing the behavior of others. They can be *unlearned,* and replaced with more workable, more nurturing methods.

Take a look again at Doris and Ben, described in the early pages of this book. Let's add a little more detail to help you understand them.

Doris and Ben have been married for almost ten years. They're a health-oriented couple: they exercise on a regular schedule, and Doris participates in aerobics twice a week. Their "presenting" problem (as clinicians call it), the problem they talk about a lot, as if it's the real issue, is that she tends to be jealous of every woman with whom he exchanges the most trivial utterances. Although she never admits it to him, she perceives him as the more attractive partner in their relationship.

Both Doris and Ben have good jobs, and they've begun to discuss starting a family. But her jealousies get in the way of their potentially good marriage, and they've hesitated to complicate it with a baby.

None of this, however, is really the essential difficulty. In a more favorable emotional climate, they could work out the answers.

They came home that night after dining out with friends, went to bed and made love. In the morning, Doris was clearly upset and accused Ben of selfishness, of not caring whether his love-making hurt her or not. "You only think about *your* needs," she complained.

In response, he accused her of never being satisfied. "I wasn't too rough at all," he insisted. "That's how I make love, okay? What do you want — a man or a dishrag?"

Then he slammed the bathroom door behind him, closing her out both physically and emotionally. At that moment, she did, indeed, feel she hated him.

The real issue at this point has almost nothing to do with the actual problem Doris and Ben are having in their sexual relations. What is in focus here is how Doris addresses the problem, and how she attempts to change Ben's behavior.

The method she used, instead of producing a responsive interest in changing, brought about only hostile and resistant feelings in him. She was trying to make him feel guilty for hurting her and deficient for thinking only of himself.

Ben's response accomplished nothing positive, either. Essentially, he blamed her for not accepting him for what he was — or, in this instance, how he performed.

As a result of this exchange — and it must be emphasized that blaming is the issue here, not the behavior that produced it — their relationship worsened. Even though Ben would (resentfully) modify his behavior, the next time they made love the emotional content of their love making would almost certainly be impaired. Resentment is often a half-step away from impotence.

Unless Doris was motivated by some unconscious desire to sabotage their marriage, she was producing consequences she actually didn't want at all, no matter how "right" she believed herself to be.

### Is There a Better Way?

Most certainly. More than one, in fact.

First, Doris could have stopped herself from confronting Ben in the middle of their wake-up activities. Not that she should have avoided the subject. On the contrary. But had she waited for a moment of tranquillity or affection between them, she might have found Ben a considerably more receptive listener.

At that time she could bring up their love-making in a more general discussion, mentioning both the good and bad in their relationship. Then the problem of physical roughness becomes a part of the whole picture (perhaps in a discussion of men's physicality in general), and not the focus for blame.

Another way might be to wait until the next time they are beginning to have sex. At that time, Doris could appropriately pull back momentarily and ask him to be gentle. "It's no fun for me when you get too rough," she might say. "I'd rather not do it at all if it's going to hurt."

The choice of method is up to her.

Her goal is to change the behavior that hurt her, and improve the relationship, not to punish Ben for the actions themselves.

In the second method described, we point out a way of using *consequences* to produce change. By pulling away, even for a moment, and saying what was suggested, Doris would make Ben aware that his roughness could result in her not wanting sex with him at all. Without resorting to blame or fault, she can still make clear that unwanted behavior produces unwanted consequences. (The use of consequences to influence behavior is a major part of No-Fault Living, and will be discussed more later on.)

Now take the second instance I presented earlier, with somewhat greater attention to detail.

Lorraine and Pete had been married 15 years. An attractive, slightly sharp-featured brunette, Lorraine has let herself get a little heavier than Pete likes, but he avoids making an issue of it, since she turned sulky and hostile when he raised it in the past, and he's balding a bit himself.

She also complains of a "bad back," and finds it difficult to lift heavy or awkward objects. Pete sometimes resents her for it, seeing it as at least partly a sympathy-grabbing pretense.

Home early from work one evening, Pete settled in his chair with the newspaper. Nearby, Lorraine struggled to fold several sets of heavy curtains she had ironed earlier.

This is the point at which the conflict situation began. Both of them handled it badly, as usual.

Tired, sweaty and angry, Lorraine asked sharply, "What's the matter with you? Can't you see this is too heavy for me? You know how my back is — don't you care at all? Why can't you *ever* show any consideration?... Give me a hand here!"

Slamming the paper down, Pete stood up and helped her finish the job, moved by a combination of guilt and resentment.

"Just put them there, please," Lorraine said coldly when they finished. Then she left the room without thanking him.

As in the case of Doris and Ben, Lorraine's words accomplished exactly the opposite of what she really wanted. Pete did get up to help her, but certainly, if Lorraine could have had her way, he would have done so out of feelings of love for her, not because he felt badgered into it, and certainly not if he was going to resent the very fact that she asked him.

For Lorraine, the immediate result (getting Pete's help) was far less important than having a happy, loving marital relationship.

Over and over again, people lose sight of what they really want in life, yielding thoughtlessly to the momentary need to find fault.

The resentment Pete felt only raised whatever barriers existed between them. The guilt he experienced could only diminish him in his own eyes — hardly an effective way to strengthen their marriage.

Input of the kind Pete received, if part of his regular emotional diet, would only make him a less enthusiastic partner. The correlation between healthy self-esteem and productive relations with others has been well established.

Yet Lorraine did seem to have cause to feel frustration, just as Doris had a right to feel annoyed that Ben was being too rough with her. The problem is not the validity of their complaints. It is, rather, how they communicated their displeasure. They could have changed the situation to their satisfaction, and done so without damaging their relationship with their husbands — maybe even bolstering it.

What might Lorraine have said?

Perhaps a direct request would have been enough: "Honey, could you give me a hand here? This is too heavy for me."

Had she done this, Pete would have had no reason to react with resentment or guilt. And, while he might have preferred not to be bothered, he could have come to his wife's help without negative feelings afterward.

If Pete's lack of consideration is a broader and more pervasive problem in their marriage, it could be the result of a certain type of upbringing. Perhaps his family hadn't stressed consideration for others. Or his insensitivity could reflect a resentment about other deficiencies in the marriage, such as Lorraine's hostility toward discussions of her weight.

But in both of the instances described, blaming and fault-finding only increase the difficulty. They could not reduce it.

If, for example, Pete did lack training in helpfulness, he might consider his responses as appropriate. Perhaps there were very few instances of his father helping his mother; perhaps his mother took care of everything. Perhaps helpfulness was rarely expected of Pete as a child. If so, blaming him here would seem to him to be unfair or even malicious.

Blame-filled admonitions directed against well-rooted attitudes tend to be self-defeating, rather than corrective.

Problems and frustrations in marriage rarely result from a single event. They are, rather, an amalgam of the life experiences of both partners — the way they solve problems, react to each other, and communicate. Too often, they develop into mutually injurious patterns.

If you think of someone or something you resent, and explore all possible reasons for that resentment, you probably will find that they stretch back over a considerable range of time and experiences.

If resentment related to other problems in the marriage is causing Pete's present inconsiderate behavior, then the roots of the resentment need to be explored. If his personal background is the cause, that too needs exploring. In the meantime, blaming can only worsen the situation.

What these relationships need is a strong dose of No-Fault Living.

*5*

# TOWARD NO-FAULT MARRIAGE

*T*he first thing that's needed in the marriages discussed in Chapter Four is an open acknowledgement that a problem exists — and that it goes beyond any specific incident. One method that has been successful for many couples is to establish scheduled, regular, semi-formal problem-solving sessions — at home.

The guidelines for these sessions are simple and straightforward. The most important consideration is that they be fully agreed on, and followed *completely,* by both partners.

1. It must be understood that the discussion will be frank and honest — but not accusatory.

2. Each partner is required to say directly what he or she wants or needs to have in order to feel satisfied about the situation under discussion.

3. Blaming is off limits. Stick to your own feelings, wants and needs. Say "I want..." and "I need...," not "You're wrong about..." or "You did..."

4. There are to be no recriminations or retaliations afterward for anything that is said during the "session." (This may be much the hardest rule to follow, but it is essential if the method is to succeed.)

Many couples find it useful to set specific time limits — perhaps five minutes — during which one partner speaks and the other listens, *without interruption or argument.* This helps prevent dominance by the louder, more verbal or more aggressive spouse.

Solutions should be offered and explored. If they can be agreed on, the necessary actions should follow. If not, the problem can be held over for discussion at the next meeting.

If particular difficulties, such as Lorraine's concern that Pete is inconsiderate *over-all,* cannot be solved in this setting without blame, then they probably would benefit from professional counseling.

But for really motivated couples, the method does work.

And for whole families, too, when they have not become too deeply mired in long-standing resentment and withdrawal. Freed of preoccupation with guilt and blame, family members often come up with sensitive and creative solutions. Ideas are explored, further emotional injuries are prevented, and deeper feelings of love and caring are freed to grow.

This is the positive potential inherent in problem-solving that totally excludes blaming. Without that negative influence — which produces at best reluctant compliance, coupled inevitably with guilt, resentment and lowered self-esteem — relationships can strengthen and build.

### *And Now, More Good News...*

In previous chapters, we've been looking at qualities that can damage a relationship, especially one as intimate and mutually dependent as marriage. But such an examination begs the far more important question: What qualities *benefit* the marriage relationship? And how are they affected by blaming and faulting?

A great deal of investigation has been done to determine what makes marriages succeed or fail. A number of traits have been identified as significant contributors. Of these, the twelve noted on the following page, a "Golden Dozen" for marital happiness, have been found by researchers to be among the most important.

Blaming and fault-finding have no place in a relationship built on these characteristics:

---

### *The Golden Dozen*

Partner qualities which increase the chances for
marital success:
1. Reasonable self-confidence and security as
   individuals;
2. The ability to care genuinely for other people;
3. Ability to assume responsibility comfortably;
4. Sensitivity to the thoughts and feelings of
   others;
5. Reasonable control over impulses, especially
   anger;
6. General optimism and cheerfulness;
7. Ability to take a leadership role, without
   needing to dominate;
8. Coorperativness and willingness to participate
   with others;
9. A sense of humor and perspective;
10. Avoidance of self-blame;
11. Generally even disposition, few extreme mood
    swings;
12. Ability to communicate in an open way, with a
    willingness to confide inner feelings.

---

### *Tricia and Harry Revisited*

Let's take another look at Tricia and Harry, the couple
whose encounter in my office opened the previous chapter.

An aggressive, successful stock broker, Harry was 35
when they married. Tricia, 24, lacked a college education
(*he* had a prestigious Master's degree in business), but she
possessed a rare combination of intelligence and beauty
that made her a conspicuously attractive mate.

The nature of Harry's business success reflected a high degree of personal insecurity. Some people are comfortable with success, and allow themselves to enjoy the fruits of their achievements. But Harry's drive had a panicky what-makes-Sammy-run quality. The offspring of unhappy, embattled parents, he used success as a club to beat off his insecurities — which kept returning to gnaw at him no matter how great his triumphs. In fact, as often happens, increased attainment brought increased fear of failing and being dragged from the heights.

Tricia's beauty, which first attracted him to her, provided him with a highly visible status symbol. But, as with his successes — which he could never feel really *belonged* to him, and never satisfactorily secured his self-esteem, — he never really trusted her attachment to him. Perennially discontented, he could not accept her as a full human being and partner in their marriage.

Because, in a fundamental way, Tricia was only an object to him, Harry made it very clear that she must always be the glamour queen he had married. If she ever appeared in public looking less than that, he found fault with her. Putting her down helped — temporarily — to shore up his own self-esteem. It allowed him to take hold momentarily of the sense of superiority her beauty lent him.

In addition, her lack of formal education provided many opportunities for him to find fault with her. Because he inhabited a professional and social sphere with many highly educated and cultivated people, he felt a need to be constantly on guard for any "slip-ups" by Tricia. If she ever offered an opinion at odds with views accepted by those around him, he publicly blamed her for not reading enough and keeping informed.

In private, he called her love-making inadequate, which he went so far as to attribute to her "lower class" background.

Although basically a giving and loving person, Tricia felt verbally and intellectually outgunned. She began to close up and withdraw. Predictably, this provoked new attacks from Harry, and the cycle became entrenched. She withdrew further. He tormented her more for it. She continued to withdraw.

Driven by frustration and humiliation, Tricia would at times try to retaliate, criticizing Harry in almost the same tone he used to attack her. While this gave her momentary relief, it only worsened the situation.

After less than a year of marriage, Harry and Tricia separated. Shortly thereafter, they were divorced.

Certainly, Harry's treatment of Tricia had neurotic roots, and she was more vulnerable in her marriage than others might have been. But their words and actions offer a clear example of the problems we've been discussing.

In view of her lesser education, Tricia came into the marriage with a notably fragile self-confidence. With her special good looks and native intelligence, she could easily have been helped to a higher level of self-esteem and self-assurance. Instead, in the damaging environment of Harry's neurotic needs, her self-confidence plummeted, and with it her ability to contribute effectively to the marriage relationship.

Eventually, she feared to take responsibility for even routine household tasks; an error was too likely to produce blame. From a basically even-tempered and cheerful person, she descended into the shadows of moodiness and depression, unwilling to take the risk of initiating activities the two of them might enjoy together.

Her sense of humor evaporated. Her original honesty in communication with Harry, when she took pleasure in opening her thoughts and feelings to him, ended in the face of his put-downs and belittlement.

When we look at the Golden Dozen traits essential to marital success, it's obvious that all of them are extremely vulnerable to the damage done by blaming and fault-finding. The qualities Tricia brought to the marriage couldn't possibly continue functioning under the belittling barrage she received.

Self-confidence, affection, cooperativeness, openness and optimism — traits waiting to bloom in Tricia with a little encouragement — wither in a hostile climate of this kind.

Without most of the Golden Dozen traits, marriage relationships tend to die on the vine, producing sour grapes instead of sweet wine.

A successful marriage may be described as one in which husband and wife are able to provide companionship — not just initial excitement and glamour. They strive to satisfy each other's most important needs. They make each other feel loved and secure.

If they can tolerate their differences, and share a variety of interests... if they can communicate openly and sincerely... if each encourages the other to grow and develop... if they are just plain *pleased* to be with each other... they have a successful marriage.

There is no place for blaming in that picture.

### And a Footnote

Just before initiating divorce proceedings, Tricia and Harry tried marriage counseling as a last resort. The severe damage caused by blaming, resentment and retaliation was explored by them. They promised to work on it, and to try to change.

But each subsequent session brought back reports that the *other* was "not really trying."

After their divorce, however, each continued in therapy, independently.

Harry's underlying needs, which resulted in compulsive blaming and fault-finding, were explored and worked on. Tricia's badly bruised self-image received a measure of restoration. In time, her ability to trust and communicate freely returned, as did her sense of humor and perspective.

Both re-married not much later. The course of their new relationships, with blaming no longer a constantly damaging force, has been considerably smoother.

Although Tricia and Harry's case is an extreme one, marriage is always an intense relationship, in which damage done by either partner causes direct reactions very quickly in the other.

### P.S.: What's The Bottom Line?

You are being asked in this book to become especially aware of the damaging effects of blaming and fault-finding, no matter how natural it may seem to use them. Part of this awareness calls for full-time consideration of "the bottom line" — the outcome you *really* desire in the long run.

Is being "right" the bottom line for you? Is making the other person feel bad the actual result you seek?

Or do you most desire an increasingly warm and loving relationship — in spite of the anger or annoyance you may feel at the moment?

Perhaps you've heard the story of the man who had a flat tire while driving down a lonely country road. Finding no jack in the trunk, Harvey set out to look for a house where he might borrow one. As he trudged along, with no house in sight, he grew more and more frustrated.

In his anger Harvey conjured up images of finally finding a farmhouse, being confronted with a skeptical farmer, and questioned about what he really wanted. He imagined a debate, then an argument. At last he actually did come upon a house. By the time the householder finally responded to his insistent knocking, Harvey had worked himself into a frenzy. He shouted, "You can keep your lousy jack!" and stalked away.

The "Bottom-Line Self-Quiz" below may help you clarify your own feelings when strong emotions threaten to push you into harmful — and probably self-defeating — blaming or faulting.

A. *Have you ever been so wound up in an argument that you ignored the consequences of what you said or did?* Harvey did just that, and stormed off without the jack he so urgently needed.

B. *Have you ever found yourself disregarding at least part of the evidence in an argument, so that you could prove yourself "right" in spite of it?* People are sometimes so busy with their own self-serving arguments that they actually miss what the other person is saying. Inner turmoil made

Harvey completely closed to anything the farmer might have said.

C. *Have you ever noticed yourself winning the argument but losing the war?* The other person "admitted" you were right, but was clearly peeved at you anyway! (Tricia and Harry are a good example. She almost always believed his put-downs of her, thought he must be right — but moved emotionally further and further away from him nonetheless.)

Keep that bottom line in mind. What do you really want: "victory" — or close and loving relationships?

# 6

## GUILT: THE LEGACY OF BLAME

$I$t has been said that the child is father to the man. What we are as adults results from what we inherited in our genes and what we experienced in our early years. The crucial role played by blaming in those years needs to be made clear. To understand this — and understand how to change that role for the better — we need to take a new look at what children are really all about, from the special perspective of No-Fault philosophy.

A human infant may be likened to a flower waiting to bud, ripen and grow. The environment that encourages the development of a flower provides warm sun, gentle rain and growth-nurturing elements from the air and soil.

Chilly temperatures, dry, harsh winds and barren soil, on the contrary, result in a withered or stunted flower.

This analogy between a person and a flower does no injury whatever to scientific accuracy. The late psychologist Carl Rogers, a towering figure in modern understanding of human behavior, made us aware of the major differences in personality development that can be produced by an attitude of *non-judgmental acceptance.* A warm, loving, no-fault environment is to the child what soft rain and gentle sunlight are to the flower.

### *"Train Up a Child..."*

Children reared by loving parents, who are consistently attentive to their needs and understanding and accepting, are encouraged to open their senses to the world, take in growth-stimulating experiences, test their abilities and seek to achieve their fullest potential.

It is vital for parents to recognize that *they* are the source of the fertile environment that encourages the child to "flower" and grow, both physically and emotionally.

The same principles of nurturing and acceptance apply to *your* relationships with friends and family. We can all flower and grow through warm, accepting, no-fault treatment of one another. Too often, however, we fail to understand these simple precepts, or we live with personal pressures so great that we are inhibited from acting on them.

How often do we hear parents saying to their children, "Not now, I'm too busy (or tired)," or "Stop that, you're bothering me!" Take a moment to consider what these words might mean to any relationship, but especially one involving a young child.

Too many parents fail to realize how little they do to help their children create a sense of self-worth, and how often they unthinkingly bruise their youngster's developing self-image. Children inevitably are irritating at times — sometimes more than irritating. But, as adults, we need to understand the importance of not striking back with accusations and blame. There are far better ways to influence children's behavior.

To experience their full potentials for growth, openness and the capacity for intimate relating, children require nurturing, caring and accepting — behaviors diametrically opposed to blaming, fault-finding and "putting down."

Parents may be merely inattentive, or they may show severity or active disregard, make inflexible demands, or cause confusion and anxiety through inconsistency. Or the problem may even take the form of serious mistreatment or cruelty. The child's natural self-protective response is, most often, to withdraw and turn inward; the child's "petals" close up, inhibiting growth and development. And the adult evolving from this child will usually continue the cycle of fault-finding, blaming, or worse, the development of significant emotional disturbance.

### *"...And When He Is Old..."*

The same psychological mechanisms that function in children operate in adults, although with greater subtlety and sophistication. While not outwardly as vulnerable as a child, an adult reacts to the psychic injury caused by blame and fault-finding in the same self-protecting ways.

None of us lead lives free of all psychic injuries; they are often beyond prevention. All we can do is learn to cope with them as effectively as possible. But inflicting emotional injury on others by fault-finding, as a consistent communications pattern, *is* preventable. We *can* do something about it.

Faulting and blaming are *learned* behaviors. They can, therefore, be *un*learned — and gain us a whole new world.

We have been exposed to the use of blame and criticism all our lives. We have become accustomed to having others tell us what we have done wrong, seeking to make us feel wrong, and therefore guilty. The specific goal of this behavior is to change us in the direction desired by the blamer, as well as to induce a tacit acknowledgement of the "rightness" of the blamer's views.

How often have you been made to feel "bad" at home, at work, in school, at church or synagogue? How often have you been made to feel "bad" for not conforming to the standards of those who have placed themselves in charge of your heart and mind?

Perhaps the cruelest irony in the almost-universal blaming and faulting of children is that almost all of us later incorporate the same tactic into our adult lives — thoughtless of the harm we are doing by repeating the pattern with our own loved ones, families, friends and colleagues in our own relationships.

We have all felt diminished in some way by being blamed. Have you ever met anyone who responded to fault-finding and blame with a glow of warmth and affection? Yet it rarely occurs to any of us to change this fundamentally destructive way of relating to others. It's as if we believe mindlessly that this harmful behavior is natural, appropriate and inevitable, when in reality it's a toxic behavior foisted on us by others.

### *"...He'll Feel Guilty"*

Blame and guilt are inseparably intertwined; they are the *yin* and *yang* of socially malignant behavior. Ever since Adam and Eve slunk from the Garden of Eden, as the Bible portrays God's blame and punishment of them for their sins, blame and guilt have haunted the human race. Regardless of which account you subscribe to, the Biblical story of man's origins or the findings of scientific anthropology, the same destructive behaviors have been a human bane as far back as history is traced.

When you blame someone, you not only seek to assign responsibility for words or deeds you would label "bad" or "wrong," you also, whether consciously or not, intend to make the other person feel guilty and obligated to change in a way you desire.

Blaming allows you to feel superior (at least in the short term), and presumably leaves the "wrongdoer" feeling remorseful, embarrassed, self-critical, resentful, and guilty. The almost universal response is an attempt to avoid pain by distancing oneself, physically and/or psychologically.

Finding fault, on the other hand, doesn't necessarily make the other person feel guilt or shame. It simply spotlights "deficiencies," although the effects can be very similar to those of blaming. Both produce negative feelings that are injurious to the person who is their object.

The story is told of a prince, abandoned in early childhood because of a fortune teller's prediction that he would one day steal his father's throne. Unaware of his ancestry, the prince did indeed eventually return to the kingdom in adulthood, taking his father's life, seizing control of the kingdom, and marrying the queen — his mother.

Upon learning the truth of his past, he blinded himself in payment for his incestuous and patricidal guilt.

You may recognize this as a modest re-telling of the ancient Greek legend of Oedipus Rex, the story upon which Sigmund Freud wrought one of his basic and most famous theories of human behavior, the Oedipus Complex.

In this theory the capacity to feel guilt is ascribed to an instinctive process elicited in children by fear and blame connected to unacceptable sexual feelings; ultimately, the guilt becomes a part of their deepest psychological selves.

Blame-induced guilt plays a constantly distorting role in our everyday lives. Oedipus' self-mutilation may not have been warranted— his was not a deliberate evil deed. It is this actual innocence that takes us to the heart of the problem we are exploring.

Guilt is mindless. It is not rational, reasonable nor logical. When guilt is produced through blame, only hateful, self-punishing feelings are aroused — feelings that can only injure, never heal.

There are, of course, certain socially appropriate uses for guilt; it can, for example, function sometimes as a deterrent against such socially harmful acts as theft or murder. But there are rarely beneficial occasions for guilt in interpersonal relationships.

There are more constructive ways to bring about change in a friend, lover, relative or colleague than to evoke guilt feelings through blame, or self-criticism through fault-finding. The injury you do to others through finding fault and assessing blame results in disadvantage to yourself as well. The effect usually is to separate you from those you love, care about or need to work with successfully: children, friends, colleagues. Certainly it does nothing to bring you closer.

Why not quit the blame game?

### P.S.: *The Blaming/Faulting Effect*

Here's another little self-examination to make clear the point of our discussion.

Think of three *actual* occasions when you were blamed for something you said or did. Ignore whether you believed you were right or wrong, good or bad. When you have three events clearly in mind, answer the following questions, True or False, for each of those three occasions:

|  | True | False |
|---|---|---|
| A. *I felt embarrassed or ashamed.* | —— | —— |
| B. *I felt guilty.* | —— | —— |
| C. *I wanted to get back at the person blaming me.* | —— | —— |
| D. *I had warmer feelings toward the other person.* | —— | —— |

Unless you have very low self-esteem or high self-blame, your answers to A, B and C will be mostly (or completely) "True": your responses to D will probably be "False" for each situation.

There may have been a difference in the intensity of your feelings of embarrassment, guilt, revenge or warmth between those occasions when you believed yourself in the right, and those when you saw yourself as wrong. But most of the time your reactions will be the same.

It is clear that, in almost all circumstances, blaming and fault-finding produce negative feelings!

# 7

## *HOW GROWN UP ARE YOU?*

*P*sychology pioneer Alfred Adler pointed out that being born tiny and helpless has an effect throughout our lives. People struggle, with more or less success, to overcome — or compensate for — the feelings that result from their early helplessness. This understanding helps explain the tendency to point a finger at the faults of others. Inducing guilt and lowered self-esteem in somebody else may help you to feel superior — temporarily — and to deny your own underlying sense of helplessness and inferiority.

Many people try to develop skills that others admire. When they succeed, they feel more secure. They seek ways to control those around them, to ensure that security. For the same reason, when they can't overcome perceived weaknesses in themselves, they try to deny them.

Teddy, a thin, studious college sophomore, had the misfortune to play the starring role in a traditionally unhappy real-life drama.

While not actually the "90-pound weakling" of the muscle-building ads, Teddy wasn't far from it. He felt the acute sense of humiliation shared by many adolescents when they see the physical powers of Rambo as ideal, and all they can offer is Woody Allen.

Teddy decided to put a stop to "having sand kicked in his face by the beach bully." He began a program designed to put on weight and muscle, trying at the same time to keep up with his studies. He followed the program diligently, punishing his body each day with bar bells and isometrics, weighing himself and studying himself in the mirror. Slowly, over time, he saw improvement.

Eventually he was forced to admit that, regardless of how hard he worked, he would always be less muscular than the bigger guys with greater natural endowment. They still cowed him, they still flexed bigger muscles and they still went out with the prettiest girls. Worse yet, his grades suffered from the diversion of his energies.

So he wisely cut back on the muscle-building, and returned his attention to his studies, where he did have the advantage of a natural aptitude. He never did connect with the girl of his beach dreams, but his drama played out well nonetheless. He fell in love with a bright, modestly attractive girl who liked and respected him for what he was. Her bubbly personality helped him accept the fact that she was no more a glamour queen than he was a muscular hunk.

But what about some other "Teddy," one who doesn't have the natural ability to redirect from brawn to brains? Or a "Teddy" who can't make himself forget the dream girls who prefer Charles Atlas to Albert Einstein? Isn't he likely to substitute bragging for actual achievement? If he gets away with it at first, and if people seem to be impressed, he may incorporate boasting into his lifestyle.

And, if boasts fail to achieve his goals, then unrelieved feelings of inferiority may continue to nag him until he tries yet another road to Rome. One of the most traveled of these is the one that says: Make psychological mincemeat of others. Put them down. Minimize them. Make them feel less worthy about themselves. And by so doing, *make yourself feel superior. Find fault with them — and feel better about yourself.*

Feel *righteous.* It's a great crutch used by many against nagging self-doubt. By labeling yourself *right* and insisting on your *goodness,* you strive to convince yourself, and others, that you are better than they. Sometimes you can fool yourself on the surface, but deep down the doubts remain, and continue to fuel the same behavioral fires.

But you can never really be warmed by such actions. You never truly augment yourself when you diminish others. The sense of gain is strictly an illusion; feelings of inadequacy and insecurity are not dispelled.

To make matters worse, the people you cause to feel diminished or guilty often are the very people you depend on ultimately for your own sense of well-being. Blaming fouls the relationship waters. Instead of nurturing connections to the important people around you, finding fault does just the opposite. All relationships suffer, a little or a lot, when blame and fault play significant roles.

The welfare of each of us depends in large part on connections to partners — spouses, lovers, parents, friends, business associates. Let's focus on ways to strengthen those connections, not weaken them.

# 8

# UNBLAMED CHILDREN AND NO-FAULT PARENTS

*A*melia didn't *want* to scream at Stuart that afternoon just before Christmas, but she couldn't help herself.

There was a mountain of last-minute shopping to do. She had hoped to get it done during the week while Stuart, her five-year-old, was at school. But errands began to pile up, and she found herself with only this last weekend to finish buying the family presents.

Amelia hated the thought of shopping on the weekend, let alone the weekend before Christmas. But she had no choice. She bundled Stuart into the car and headed for the mall, thinking she would make it a treat for him. They would visit with Santa, have pizza for lunch, shop, and then come home.

Then the irritations began. The line to visit Santa was long and slow-moving — at least a forty-minute wait. Although she tried to dissuade Stuart, he was adamant. So they waited and he made his gift demands to Santa. Then the pizza was cold and he wouldn't eat it. The stores were packed. By the time they finally headed back to the car it was four-thirty, and her arms were loaded with heavy packages.

"Hold on to my coat, Stuart," she said wearily, as they started across the parking lot. "I can't hold your hand." She glanced over her packages to make sure he was listening. He was walking quietly enough. Maybe he was as tired as she was. But suddenly, seeing their car at a distance, he darted out into the traffic lane. She shouted frantically, but he didn't even look back. A car zoomed down the aisle, missing him by inches.

"Come back here, you little brat!" Amelia screamed, dropping her packages. "Come back here or I'll *kill* you!" She felt her face flush, knowing the people hurrying by were looking at her. She knew too that she hardly sounded like one possessed of the holiday spirit. But the words spilled out unchecked. "Wait till I'm *dead* because of you. You'll be sorry! You lousy kid, get back here right now or I'll break every bone in your body!"

Tired, frustrated and panicked, her words spewed out — harsh and violent, expressions of fear converted to rage, without room for any thought of their effect on Stuart. A caring, loving mother, at that moment she sounded as though she despised her son.

Then, catching up with him, and more conscious of onlookers' eyes, she hissed in his ear, "What did I do that

God punishes me like this? You'll be sorry when I'm dying in bed because of you!"

Tirades like this seem unlikely and ridiculous when we look at them in print. But, like many parents, Amelia often used such words when she felt she'd lost control. A great many mothers use words equally harsh, sometimes for a lot less reason — put-down words, frightening words, words of blame or guilt. Most of these women truly love their children. But loving or not, their abusive language often damages the youngsters' undeveloped and vulnerable self-esteem.

It's an interesting — and a little scary — psychological fact that children tend to think of themselves in the terms their parents use to describe them. Most adults have little awareness of the damage that guilt-producing blame, however unthinkingly employed, can do to children of any age. Children usually are not able to discount verbal attacks, nor allow for the intense emotions that produce them.

Mothers are not alone in such actions, of course. Fathers often do much the same thing.

Take Tom, a generous, humorous man, an interested, participating father. He heads his son's Scout troop, gets involved in his schooling, coaches his junior baseball team.

Last year his son's team, the "White Sox," came close to the league championship. All they had to do was beat the "Dodgers." With the score tied in the last inning, Tom's son Mickey was pitching. An error by the shortstop put the lead-off batter on first, and the runner advanced to second on a sacrifice bunt. Mickey struck out the next batter.

With two out, and the clean-up hitter moving to the plate, Tom yelled, "Put him on, son. We'll get the next one!"

Mickey later insisted he hadn't heard his father. Whatever the reason, his first pitch split the plate, waist high — and was promptly driven into the gap between center and left field. The run scored easily.

Tom stormed to the mound. "What's the matter with you?" he screamed. "Don't you *ever* listen to me? If we don't win the championship — *it's all your fault!*"

Mickey walked the next two batters, and then allowed another double before Tom pulled him from the mound, again blaming him intemperately for the team's misfortunes.

This was not the first time Tom's own competitive zeal had badly bruised his son's self-esteem. Losing the championship was nothing next to the psychological damage Tom had caused — so much so that Mickey refused to go out for baseball the following year.

### Parenting Can Be Hard Work

Not many parents have sons or daughters in position to win a junior championship. But nearly all parents find themselves confronted with frequent opportunities to hurt their children as Tom did Mickey. It can be a difficult challenge.

Like a lot of eight-year-olds, Ingrid's son Philip frequently fails to live up to her expectations of even minimal social behavior. Invariably, when Philip comes up short, Ingrid berates him with such classic put-downs as: "Why can't you be like Henry? He's always polite to grown-ups. He does what his parents tell him. He pays attention in school." Etc., etc., etc. Unfortunately, such tirades are serving only to drive Philip away from his mother, not to improve his social skills.

Verbal abuse, whether of the type used by Amelia, Tom or Ingrid, almost always injures self-esteem — and *rarely* induces willing cooperation or teaches more desirable behavior. But most parents do it, at least some of the time.

Parenting *is* difficult for almost everyone. Most children are at times frustrating, aggravating, tiring, disappointing... and delightful... or in-between. How we react to the problems of parenting significantly influences the adults our children become.

Too often, we expect children to act like adults — and perfect adults at that.

Becoming a biological parent is a relatively simple task. But becoming a *good* parent, an *effective* parent, is more difficult than most people are aware.

In some circles, parenthood (especially motherhood) is endowed with a nearly sacred status. To most of us, "mom" (like apple pie?) occupies a special place on a special pedestal, producing a blindly sentimental knee-jerk reflex whenever the image is presented. Mothers and fathers are seen as having an almost divine sanction to rear *their* children in whatever way they consider best, short of actually abusing them physically.

But parental ignorance is, too often, abysmally deep. The same people you might not trust for five minutes as caretakers of *your* children are unconditionally credited by society with the ability to do right by their own.

It has been suggested that both parenting and marriage, in our complex world today, require more skill and knowledge than most of us possess instinctively. We need to *think* and *learn,* to be effective as parents and as partners.

It is the parent who must bear the brunt of the responsibility for the child's healthy growth and development. The parent provides the model on which the child bases most assumptions of "good" and "bad" behavior, both consciously and unconsciously. The parents' relationship with each other demonstrates daily what relationships between people can be like — especially when it comes to the difference between accepting and blaming.

### Children's Needs and Parents' Deeds

Particularly vital in understanding children is an awareness of *needs,* and their relationship to no-fault living. As we've noted earlier, security needs and acceptance needs are crucially important in all of us, but most especially in children.

Consider June, now forty-two years old and married to Sol. She has vivid memories of her childhood and of her mother, almost all of them unhappy. She remembers herself at age ten, being told by her mother that, "You're too fat... too dark... too stupid... too selfish..." If it was unfavorable, June's mother accused her of it. Yet she *cared* for June, saw herself as a loving mother, and praised her daughter to others. Her personal history of self-doubt made it impossible for her to be accepting of her daughter.

The constant criticism continued into June's adolescence. According to her mother, June didn't have any taste in clothes, didn't know how to use make-up, didn't know how to relate to boys, didn't have much of anything worth having.

June's marriage is on the rocks primarily because she "bought" her mother's perceptions of her, even as she rebelled against them during her teen years. High in self-blame and low in self- esteem, June puts herself down when talking to her husband and puts down their 12-year-old daughter, Donna, when talking to her.

To Donna, June's words are like a taped replay of her grandmother's words to her mother. Sometimes Donna notes that her mother's voice even sounds like her grandmother's.

Discussing this, June notes, "I know I'm doing it. I hear myself saying it. But I can't help it — that child is so frustrating!" She continues to deny the reality that her nagging *causes* Donna's frustrating behavior.

Sol has become so incensed by what he sees happening to his daughter that the marriage has become a verbal battleground, even in areas unrelated to the problem. When Donna is with her father, she tries to get as close as possible, seeking comfort and security. But when she is with her mother, her personality changes to teary, complaining, sullen withdrawal or outright defiance.

Only if June can change the patterns drilled into her by her own blaming, fault-finding mother can she hope to establish a warm and rewarding relationship with her daughter and husband.

Child care experts often urge that parents avoid calling their children down in front of the youngsters' friends. This is most powerfully true for adolescents, in whom peer pressure sensitivity is at its height. Finding fault or putting blame on teenagers in front of their friends can, for some, be devastating.

The major point is always the same. How can we encourage our children to develop good feelings about themselves, and grow up with a reasonable supply of life-coping self-confidence, yet pull in the reins on their misbehavior? When we *accept,* instead of finding fault, we make possible fulfillment of one of the most basic needs of humankind: the need to build security feelings in an ever-pressuring world.

Children have many other needs, as well, varying to some extent with each individual. They need physical nurturance, of course — and emotional nurturance, too. That means they need to be loved (very much the opposite of being blamed). Research indicates that, on the average, lovingly nurtured children actually grow physically larger and stronger than those who have been emotionally deprived.

Children need to have opportunities to learn about the world, to try their skills, to develop ways of dealing effectively with the people and things around them... without holding back out of fear of being shamed or blamed.

They need to feel *understood* — which means they need to be *listened to.*

Parents are human and therefore inconsistent. One minute you're loving and supportive; the next you're annoyed and irritable. Children don't understand these changes – unless you explain your feelings. Take time to help your child(ren) *make sense* of the world (including parental inconsistencies).

### *What Do You Want Them To Be Like?*
A list of the qualities most of us would like our children to have would probably include the following:

- *The capacity for loving and caring*
- *Reasonable self-confidence*
- *The ability to feel comfortable with other people*
- *Goal-oriented views and attitudes*
- *The ability to live within the requirements of society*
- *An interest in making the most of their potential*
- *Consideration and concern for the well-being of others*
- *Willingness to take responsibility*
- *Good emotional adjustment*

It's obvious that blaming and fault-finding can only have a destructive effect on the development of these qualities.

### *Tips and Tactics For No-Fault Parenting*

Children can be demanding, irritating and self-centered. No doubt about it. In some ways, this is the very nature of childhood. But rewards in parenting are greatest when children bloom into adults who feel *good* about themselves and the world they live in.

You can help that happen — without being lax or overpermissive. Here are some suggestions for parents and plan-to-be parents:

- *Pay attention* to what the child is saying, not just to what *you* want of the child.

- Try to *understand the child's needs.* If you can satisfy them in an appropriate way, try to do so. If satisfying a need would be wrong for the child's welfare, or harmful to others, *explain* why you cannot do so. (If the child is too young to understand, you may need to take a stand against some demands without it being clear to the child why, but it still helps the child feel respected if you make the effort. And respect encourages growth.)

• Once you take a position, *be open to valid reasons for changing your mind* — but stick to your guns otherwise. Do so quietly and firmly. Be more grown-up than your children — give them something good to model after. Yelling and screaming, or using superior force to inflict pain in order to produce compliance, merely brings you down to their level, and teaches the child such behavior is acceptable.

• When you expect something to be done, *explain* — again — *what you want,* simply and clearly. Do so *in advance,* not afterward in anger when they fail. *Don't assume they know,* then blow your top because they don't.

• *Make sure the consequences of not cooperating are clearly defined* — again, *in advance.* Small punishments should be specified for first violations. These can include merely your expressed displeasure (which may be enough for a sensitive child), or such penalties as loss of a half hour of TV watching, or a small one-time reduction in allowance. When a penalty is promised, make sure it is imposed if called for. Otherwise, you are being unfair and creating an inconsistent world for your child.

Further violations of the same rule or requirement are followed by moderately increasing — but always pre-explained — additional penalties. It's worth repeating many times: *Consequences determine behavior.*

• *Rewards for desired cooperative behavior* are even more important. Some parents have the strange notion that a child's cooperation is to be expected, and only non-compliance should have consequences. Children only know what they learn. Rewarded behavior becomes learned behavior, as behavioral psychologists have demonstrated over and over.

Rewards can be praise, expressions of appreciation, extra privileges, gifts, even small amounts of money. I have heard parents complain that this is "bribery." If true, then being paid for working at a job is also bribery. Most people go to work only because they are paid. They are, then, being "bribed" every time they receive a pay check! (The true meaning of bribery is payment to induce wrongdoing.)

The goal, of course, is cooperative behavior for its own sake. This becomes the child's *learned pattern,* as a result of two considerations: (1) Awareness at some level that the behavior is *appropriate* and *makes sense,* and (2) Rewarding consequences result from it.

Blaming is a kind of consequence, too. The wrong kind. Too many parents use it as a primary form of child control. Then they expect the *desired* behavior to appear in their children as if by magic.

All the people in this chapter — Amelia and her son Stuart, Ingrid and Philip, Tom and Mickey, June and her daughter Donna — exemplify the deeply destructive nature of parental blaming and faulting. Such tactics can be used to control, for the moment at least. But their ultimate effect is to *destroy.*

As parents, let us seek to *build.*

### P.S.: *Childhood Personality and the Blaming/Faulting Syndrome*
Here's another small exercise that may make what we're talking about more meaningful to you.

Take another look at the list on page 55 of qualities

most people would like their children to have. If you have children of your own, ask yourself how they rate on these qualities. How have your children's experiences in-fluenced these qualities in them — especially blaming or faulting?

Stop and think about each of the items in the list. Be rigorously honest. Use the rating scale below; it will help keep you objective.

If you don't have a child, rate *yourself* as you remember yourself in childhood. Try to relate the results to experien-ces you had with being blamed or faulted in your own younger days.

If the rating is low for one or more qualities, you may be able to see how blaming or fault-finding caused that effect. If it's high, you may be able to see how praise and acceptance were major factors in the result.

Finally, pick two or three of the items you may have rated low, and begin today to work at raising it by praise and acceptance (of your child and/or yourself)!

# 9

## *FAULT-FREE FRIENDS AND LOVERS*

*T*he most difficult relationships for many of us are those with friends and lovers.

That is not to say that marital and parent-child relationships are easy! But our family ties are established by the original family structure and the customs of marriage. Mothers and fathers can fall back on traditional roles in establishing patterns of interaction with their children; brothers and sisters have fairly clear positions within the family structure, as do husbands and wives.

Friendships and romantic relationships, however, offer such a wide range of potentials that structuring them is often difficult.

Friends and lovers often must start "from scratch" in defining their relationships. Additionally, many people find intimacy threatening. Without a clear family structure to direct their behavior, they sometimes create an "intimacy anxiety" that stands in the way of closeness and warmth.

And many people bring to a love relationship an excess of difficult "baggage."

Sherry and Len's story is a good example. Both are 38 years old and both have been married and divorced.

Len is a stocky, rather homely man, with a master's degree in sociology. He has been working as a high school teacher and continuing to study for his doctorate. Because he perceives himself as unattractive, he tends to be over-sensitive. Perhaps by way of compensation, he has developed a personality that comes across as unusually polite and thoughtful.

His divorce three years ago was a terribly damaging experience for Len. The division of property was hotly contested, and especially painful because his two adolescent children sided with their mother. Besides severing the marriage, he also withdrew from regular contact with his children.

Sherry is a very pretty brunette, about Len's height, with a soft, obliging manner. Unlike Len, her divorce was amicable. She shares custody of her two children with her ex- husband, and remains on good terms with him, sometimes relying on his advice when making financial decisions. She is very close to her children, a girl of twelve and a boy of nine.

Sherry and Len teach at the same school, where they first met during a faculty lunch. In the familiar and safe setting of the faculty room, they were able to talk and get to know each other. They saw themselves as kindred souls struggling through similar life problems.

By the end of the term, Sherry and Len had a steady arrangement; they saw each other at least one night during the week and every Saturday or Sunday — occasionally both. Although they spent considerable time together, their physical relationship remained tentative and incomplete. They could best be described as friends-going-on-lovers.

One Saturday, four months into their relationship, they planned to meet at two in the afternoon at her garden apartment, to which she'd recently given him a key. It was a warm, spring afternoon and Len arrived early, looking forward to a pleasurable day and evening. When he let himself in, he found a note from Sherry on the hall table: "Got word unexpectedly I'd be able to spend some time today with the kids. Went to the zoo. Will drop them off with their father around two-thirty. Be back by three. *Please Wait!*... Love, Sherry."

Len settled down in the living room and began to wait, at first patiently, then gradually with annoyance. "I wouldn't change *my* plans to be with kids," he told himself at first. "But okay, we're different that way. She's entitled."

But such judicious feelings soon gave way to resentment. "Why didn't she make arrangements to be back by two?" He wondered why she was placing time with her children over time with him. He began to wonder whether she was playing some kind of hard-to-get game with him.

By three o'clock he was pacing the floor and impatiently consulting his watch. Sherry arrived at five after three, breathless from rushing. She smiled a pleased greeting when she saw he had waited, but her smile quickly evaporated at the expression on his face.

"This," he sputtered, barely concealing his anger. "This," he repeated, waving the note in the air, "was very unfair."

"I'm sorry," Sherry began, but Len cut her off.

"We have so little time together as it is. Obviously, that isn't very important to you. Did it occur to you how much I was looking forward to this afternoon? Or did you only think about yourself?"

Sherry felt her face flush in anger. She took a deep breath to control herself. "I tried to get you on the phone several times after I heard from the children," she explained. "But there was no answer.

"If you want to know the truth, Len, it's you who's being unfair. I could have spent the entire day with my kids, but I arranged to cut it short, so we could have the afternoon together."

She hesitated then plunged on. "I love my kids. It's that simple. I'm sorry you don't have a satisfying relationship with *your* children, but that's not my fault. Just don't try to keep me from being mother to my kids because of it!"

The exchange left them both distant and thoroughly unromantic for the rest of the day. By mutual agreement, they called off the date early in the evening.

They both refrained from calling the next day, though both wanted to. By Monday, they were uncomfortably avoiding each other at school. Although they managed to patch things over by mid-week, their relationship had been irreparably damaged.

Both Len and Sherry were accustomed to blaming in their relationships and, being articulate people, they were adept at subtle verbal injury. As time went on, their romance gradually faded. Sherry eventually met someone else and remarried.

Could Len and Sherry have handled the situation differently? Let's explore it a bit.

First, it's important to differentiate valid resentments and criticisms from blame and fault-finding. There *was* a degree of validity to Len's feelings; they did have plans for the afternoon. However, the accusation that she was "unfair" and the way he waved the note in her face served only to arouse hurt and anger in her.

And, of course, considering Sherry's feelings for her children, it was valid for her to take advantage of an opportunity to be with them, even if it did require a scheduling change for her date with Len. However, responding to his hurt by faulting his relationship with *his* children hardly reduced the tensions between them.

How to rewrite the script? We could start by having Len communicate his feelings *without* attacking. His words might have been: "I have to tell you, I'm really ticked off! I feel hurt because it appears I'm not important to you. I wish you had at least let me know when you found out your kids were coming. I was really looking forward to this day with you!"

There is no blaming in this statement, only a personal complaint about feeling angry and hurt, based on the incorrect assumption that Sherry hadn't tried to get in touch with him; then he ended on a positive note.

With that lead, Sherry wouldn't have felt boxed in a corner, having to defend her feelings for her children versus her feelings toward Len. Her reply?

"I'm really sorry, Len. I've been looking forward to being with you, too. But we can still have the day — minus only an hour. I did try to call you. I would never change our plans without trying to get in touch with you. But you must have been out.

"You *are* important to me. I cut my time with the kids as short as possible. I've been looking forward to today all week, but please realize I need to have as much contact with my kids as possible. Come on — let's start over and enjoy the rest of the day!"

In this exchange, both Len and Sherry clearly communicate their feelings, but without the damaging inclusion of blame and fault-finding.

Examine the two exchanges carefully again. Note that there are concrete differences in *what* was communicated, not just in *how* it was done. The issue does not concern social graces or superficial word changes. Using "nice" words instead of harsh ones doesn't alter what you really communicate. If you intend to blame someone, that will come through, no matter how sugar-coated the language you use.

The key point here is that you need to be *aware* of how you respond to disappointment. Were you brought up to use blaming and faulting as a primary method of influencing others? Use your awareness of yourself to monitor and change attitudes and behavior patterns that stand in the way of the relationships you really want.

## *Hurtful Criticism Can Cost*

Blaming takes the warmth out of any affectional relationship, whether it involves lovers, "friends-going-on-lovers" or less intense connections. For example:

Jackie and Connie met as high school seniors. Both were extremely bright and highly motivated. Both intended to go to law school after college, and both planned to specialize in international law.

Their similarities were striking. "Proper" family backgrounds, law ambitions, academic talent — they even *looked* alike (both small with brownish-blonde hair worn long). Constantly together, they were known in school as "the Siamese twins."

Everything seemed in place for Jackie and Connie to enjoy a warm enduring friendship. But a serious problem was brewing. Jackie was an "I-can't-be-wrong" person, an attitude she developed early in life as a defensive response to her perfectionist father's unstinting demands.

This attitude was soon focused on Connie. If they went on a double date and the boys failed to call them again, Jackie said it was because Connie had "clowned around too much." If they arrived late to a party because Jackie, driving, had gone down the wrong road, it was Connie's fault for failing to remind her where to make the correct turn.

When Connie finally tired of being a pin cushion, she began to return the barbs. A sharper tone entered their conversations, which soon deteriorated into "ranking out" sessions, usually begun by the more aggressive Jackie. Boys who interested Connie were labelled "creeps." Even Connie's looks were belittled.

"You're not really going to wear those jeans, are you?"

Jackie might ask, gesturing towards Connie's boyish rear end. "You look like Tommy" (Jackie's kid brother).

Connie would retaliate, "Don't you think you should pull your belly in? You stand like a fat old lady!"

"Maybe I don't stand up like a stick," Jackie might retort. "But you're so flat *all* over — you look like a boy!"

While "ranking out" — use of the "friendly" put-down — is a typical teen-age practice, this was an emotionally different exchange, motivated by growing anger on both sides.

Their friendship died long before graduation.

### *Tennis, Anyone?*

Trustworthy behavior strengthens the bond that ties good friends together. Fault-finding and blaming are among the most potent examples of *un*trustworthy behavior. We often see the bonds of solid friendship formed on the playing field, but unfortunately that is also a place where friendships can be destroyed.

Tim and Clark are two young real estate brokers who met at a tennis academy. They began a friendship both needed and wanted, since they had recently arrived from other towns. One day they were playing doubles against a somewhat more skilled pair of opponents... and losing.

Clark, a born athlete, played the way he lived, impatiently and competitively. Tim, more intellectual than athletic, usually moved slowly and cautiously.

Half-crouched at the net, Tim watched a high lob sail over his head. Reacting late, he chased it half-heartedly, coming up short. Clark's tolerance level, modest at best, gave way.

"Don't you ever *hustle*?" he snapped. "If you'd *moved*, you'd have gotten it."

Embarrassed by the criticism, and defensive about his lack of athletic prowess, Tim offered a lame excuse. "I lost it in the sun."

"Yeah, right. Come on," Clark urged. "Let's get them this time."

Tim felt a surge of dislike for Clark. He hated the rah-rah attitude. And he hated feeling like a klutz, which is how he felt whenever he played with Clark. The rest of the set, Tim pressed too hard, missing easy shots, slapping balls into the net or overshooting the court.

After that day, he began to find excuses not to respond to Clark's tennis invitations. Since Clark's impatience extended to other parts of their friendship, so did Tim's growing resentment...until he soon found reasons to end the relationship altogether.

Clark felt a vague sense of having done something wrong as Tim withdrew, but he wasn't sure what. He had had several other friendships evaporate in a similar fashion.

If Tim had found it possible to be honest enough to point out the source of his resentment, perhaps Clark could have changed his relationship style. If Clark had been made aware of the damage his manner caused, he *could* have said, in a situation like the one with the missed lob, "Tough luck, Tim. You'll get it next time."

However, given his competitiveness, that reaction may be unlikely. He might have said something more like, "Tim, I think you ought to play back more. Let me take the net shots most of the time."

This would have lessened the burden on Tim's modest skills, and given their friendship an opportunity to grow.

Friendship tends to involve less sensitive feelings than those in a love relationship. The intensity of lovers' passion, along with their usual tendency to idealize each other, sometimes overcomes the effects of blame and assessment of fault. Friendships rarely have that cushion. When friends transgress, there is often no way to minimize the injury and save the relationship.

Warm, trusting relationships are rarer than most of us would like. However, when patterns of blaming and faulting can be overcome, when openness and intimacy are felt safe, friends who might otherwise remain protectively wary have the opportunity to become close and special.

# 10

## HOW TO SUCCEED IN BUSINESS WITHOUT REALLY BLAMING

$\mathcal{B}$lame causes as many problems in business relationships as in every other relationship in our lives. This is true whether the business is on the eighty-second floor of a great banking institution or in the kitchen of a neighborhood donut shop. In business, even more than at home or school, the results of either a productive or damaging relationship can be concretely assessed and measured, directly and easily, through profit and loss.

A large banking institution once used a television commercial that showed a middle-level manager approaching the door of his superior's office. A portly, well-fed gentleman, the manager is self-confident and jaunty as he knocks and enters. A moment later, we hear the booming voice of his boss from behind the closed door, caustically dressing him down for his stupidity in placing the company account in a bank that does not pay interest on checking (unlike the sponsor of the commercial).

Then the door opens, and out slinks the cowed figure of the same manager, *now shown about one-fifth his former size.*

Vividly and graphically, this image depicts the effect of blaming in the world of business. Yes, someone is "cut down to size." But unlike the superficial sense of justice such an action might connote to some, the overall effect on the employee can be severely damaging.

What might have been the effect on our television manager if he were a real-life employee?

We may assume that he scurries back to his desk, terrified that his job — perhaps his whole career — may be in jeopardy. Shakily, he hastens to switch his company's account to an interest-paying bank. That night, he goes home worrying about his *faux pas*, re-living his dressing down and agonizing about his future with the company.

Unless something significant and immediate happens to refurbish his self-confidence, this executive now may tremble over every decision he makes, worry obsessively about what his superiors think of him, and live with constant anxiety — all of which can only decrease his effectiveness and competence at his job.

Managing well, at any level, requires the ability to make decisions and to lead. That ability is crippled by confidence- destroying blame or caustic fault-finding.

Taking the lead in the early stages of any activity, no matter how profitable it seems to be, becomes an almost intolerably risky experience. Doubts take over. "What if I'm wrong again?" becomes the operative thought.

Instead of clear thinking, creative planning and vigorous initiative, the manager finds himself playing it safe, relying on the conventional rather than on original thinking.

Foolish planning and poor decisions cannot go unchallenged. No business could succeed with that policy. By the same token, no business needs to keep a manager (or any other employee) who constantly makes serious mistakes. If the employee is seen as an important member of the company staff, why blame or find fault if he or she makes an occasional mistake? Why not take the opposite tack? Make sure the problems that are part of the job are clearly defined. Establish modes of participation, rather than exclusion, through which the person can learn and improve. Invite consultation with superiors when the stakes are high.

How much more effective it is when your boss says, "I don't blame you for mis-handling that problem, since it was new. Here's how I want you to take care of it next time..." The boss is expressing confidence in you, even as you are made aware that you did something wrong.

This approach makes it possible for you to reply, "Thanks for the advice. It makes sense. I appreciate your help."

In the business setting, warm feelings aren't the goal; successful and profitable relationships are. However, as any successful manager and executive can attest, creating

a feeling of warm acceptance produces a far more productive environment than put-downs.

Again, merely sugar-coating criticism is not what I'm
talking about. That never works. Not at home, not at work.
The point is that other approaches work *better*.

A senior art director at a large advertising agency was
known for the tactics he used to critique his staff's work.
Looking at a specific layout or illustration, he would
glance at the artist and say, "You know, I think you're one
of the most creative people we have; I expect you to fill my
shoes one of these days," or words to that effect. Then he
would verbally shred the work to bits. And he wondered
why his department suffered from a high rate of resigna-
tions.

When errors must be pointed out, the wise supervisor
notes them as a statement of fact, *not* as a means of
diminishing the worker, and suggests corrections rather
than pillorying the offender. If the worker is worth having
on the team, it pays to improve — not tear down — his or
her ability to function.

Taking employees into planning and decision-making,
to whatever extent is practical, significantly improves
work performance at all levels of the organization. The
message clearly is the same as elsewhere in this book:
Injury to self-esteem, by *blaming* and *fault-finding*,
results in decreased performance. Respect and encouragement increase it.

This no-fault principle applies to all aspects of business. Are you a boss dealing with employees? Or an
employee dealing with a boss? Do your on-the-job relationships involve other employees at your own level, in a crew,
work team or management group? Are your main business

relationships with customers? Or are you a customer dealing with suppliers (as a housewife buying groceries or a manufacturer ordering components from a supplier)?

All business relationships, can be mauled by the "natural" human practices of blaming and finding fault.

Employees who see themselves as unfairly treated have been known to respond toward their employers with blameful invective, often courting prompt dismissal. In cases like these, the folly of blame is obvious. On the other side, bosses who have used fault-finding or blame on workers have, in some extreme cases, been assaulted by resentment-crazed employees. However infrequent, such instances illustrate the general principle that severely injuring the self-esteem of another person never serves a useful purpose.

Poor morale, increasing conflict, and inattention to the needs of business often result from conflict in the workplace. There are successful ways to resolve interpersonal problems, but blaming and fault-finding must be explicitly ruled out.

Contrary to the title of the famous comedic play and movie, *How to Succeed in Business Without Really Trying,* succeeding in business is not easy. Success takes a lot of "trying." It requires determination and persistence, diplomacy and tact, initiative and leadership, clarity of thought and concentrated attention. All of these are impaired when your ego is bruised and your anxiety is raised by being accused or found deficient.

Often the resulting damage to the business is direct and obvious. Sometimes it is more subtle.

Cynthia had recently been promoted to personnel manager at a small insurance company after fifteen years of dedicated service. She was elated with the promotion, and she worked hard to succeed at her new post.

She had occasion to hire a young man at an entry level position; he wasn't an exceptional candidate on paper, but he impressed her with his apparent sincerity and desire to do a good job. His ideas seemed interesting and so, although she had some misgivings about gaps in his background, she hired him.

Within a month Cynthia and her boss discovered that the young man was a drug user and had been stealing from the petty cash drawer. Cynthia's sense of personal responsibility placed a heavy weight on her.

Her boss compounded the damage. "Don't you *screen* people?" he boomed, and followed this with a tirade about managerial carelessness and ineptitude.

Like our TV-commercial manager earlier, Cynthia's reaction to her boss's tirade was to become increasingly anxious about her job. And the consequences of her anxiety were revealed in the nature of the personnel she hired.

She became guarded in her decisions, often taking on "safe" plodders rather than creative young men and women, because the plodders were more easily justified on paper.

With the influx of these unimaginative employees, the company itself became plodding rather than creative, with inevitable consequences in the profit and loss columns — and the boss couldn't quite put his finger on the cause.

In addition, Cynthia came to see her own position as nothing but a nine-to-five grind, and she began to hate it.

A successful business or work environment depends on personal relationships. Communication is the key to those relationships, just as to any other. Fault-finding and blaming are too often behaviors that poison these relationships and foster misunderstanding. The resulting poor morale, increased conflict among workers, and loss of respect for superiors leads to reduced productivity, lower customer satisfaction, and less profit.

If Cynthia's boss handled things incorrectly, the manager of a fast food restaurant handled things much better.

A customer made abrasive comments to the girl at the cash register. Overhearing the remarks, the youth at the grill told the customer where he could go, in equally intemperate terms. The manager stepped in before the incident could escalate, but he felt a need to discipline his employee without putting him down.

First, he took time to go over the incident with the young man, discussing other possible ways of handling it. Then he decided to post a sign in the kitchen, so that all the workers would know he was prepared to support them even in difficult circumstances. It read: "THE CUSTOMER IS ALWAYS RIGHT. BUT WE RESPECT YOUR RIGHTS, TOO. LET'S TALK."

At year's end, his franchise won a regional award for efficiency and courtesy.

Cooperation, support, encouragement — these are the modes of relating to others which produce constructive and profitable relationships in business, as in all other human activities.

How about this "sign" by the door: "PLEASE PARK BLAME AND FAULT OUTSIDE."?

# 11

## *THE GOLDEN AGE OF NO-FAULT LIVING*

*S*ome people look forward to their older years as an opportunity, at long last, to get out of the rat race, do the things they've always wanted to do and enjoy life. Others view the prospect of growing older with apprehension, seeing it as a time when the pleasures of youth are lost forever.

Regardless of your expectations, the "golden years" will arrive, and for too many — they aren't particularly golden.

Time and energy spent struggling against insecurities and anxieties waste the years that could afford you the greatest enjoyment and freedom. Why do these years become so tarnished for many of us?

At age 58, Lester took disability retirement from his job with the city fire department. Although he had a frequently painful spinal disk problem — and had been doing desk work as a result — he was otherwise physically fit and was looking forward to his retirement with great expectations.

He imagined fishing trips with friends. He pictured taking the camper and traveling with his wife on a long jaunt across the country. Married when he was 36 and Sylvia was 29, Lester often felt they missed out on being young together. He planned his retirement to make up for that lost opportunity.

But then came the question of Sylvia leaving her job. She had gone back to work as an executive secretary when their sons were in junior high school, and her earnings had made a significant difference to their income. From the beginning, Lester and Sylvia had decided that as much of her salary as possible would be used to pay for college tuition. Giving that salary up now didn't seem feasible. Lester's pension could never guarantee their children's education.

Still, Lester remained optimistic. "We'll just travel during your vacation time. Maybe we can even pool it with a couple of sick days..." That and weekend trips would be almost as good, he thought.

Then it turned out that most of his friends were still too busy with their own jobs and marriages to spare much time for camping and fishing. Disappointed by how far short reality fell from his expectations, Lester settled for attending more ball games (which, unfortunately, aggravated his back condition), puttering about the garden and watching too much television.

Without the distraction his job had given him, Lester found himself suffering from more, not less, back pain. He became more anxious about his condition, worrying if he would need back surgery. The prospect of an operation opened a Pandora's box of worries.

Sylvia began to complain that he was becoming "crotchety," hardly a term he had ever envisioned being applied to himself. She said he was *blaming* her too much for trivial shortcomings.

Their children began shortening their visits home from college because Lester found fault with everything from their study habits to the way they talked and dressed. He began to complain that they were "neglectful children."

As these irritations began to snowball, Lester's retirement became an actively unhappy experience for him and everyone around him.

Many of the developments that plagued Lester's retirement seem to go with the territory — the aging territory.

### How To Become An Old Fogey

If you're older than fifty, you may well be asking yourself questions such as these:

Is it too late for me to get the things I've always really wanted in life?

Are illness and physical decline all I have to look forward to?

Is my sex life all downhill from now on?

Are people starting to see me as a less valuable person?

Do they take me less seriously and treat me with less esteem and respect?

How do I deal with the reality that the end of my existence is getting a bit too close for comfort — too close to keep hiding it from myself? What happens to me when that time really comes?

These and questions like them trouble many people by the time they reach fifty, and most people by age sixty. The reality is that, in today's society, old age has been pushed back anywhere from ten to twenty years. The physical and mental powers that began to decline by age fifty a generation or two ago now don't start to wane until sixty or seventy — for some people even later than that.

But the *feelings* about growing older which show up at age fifty or so haven't changed much. It's the way we *feel* about those questions, and certainly the way people confront them and attempt to deal with them, that can make later-life relationships unsuccessful — or deeply rewarding and fulfilling.

These may be the relationships that were the most important during earlier years, or they may include some developed more recently. With youthful vigor and activity now a part of life for many even into the sixth and seventh decades, with new friendships formed, even new marriages and family relationships, these are the years to greet life's experiences, more than ever, with "wise eyes" that recognize the drawbacks of old ways.

While the "marker" varies — whether fifty or sixty or sixty-five — most people reach a time when they no longer can hide from what they've been refusing to face for most of their lives: they are *mortal*.

Many develop a pervasive undercurrent of anxiety or

depression, that too often articulates itself in the way they relate to others.

Sometimes they become obsessively involved with inner anxieties. Any sign of weakness or illness carries with it the threat of ultimate doom. They focus on themselves. This focus might seem reasonable to them, but from the outside it appears that they are selfish and self-centered.

Sometimes they isolate themselves, not wanting to reveal newly intrusive deficiencies. They believe no one younger could possibly understand what they are going through.

Yet, often, they reach out for assurance that they are loved. They become demanding, finding symbolic weight in every gesture, measuring each action and word to see if they are still cared about. The more anxiety-ridden might ask: Will I be protected when my ability to cope with life's daily events becomes seriously weakened?

People who focus on such trivial actions and give them so much meaning can't help but become overly sensitive about the slights and oversights of others.

They complain if grown children don't call regularly. They complain if grandchildren have activities they prefer over spending time with them. They complain if they don't receive "enough" understanding or concern when they mention an ache or pain.

These manifestations often become an increasing source of worry or irritation to others. The complainers seem to be bothersome "old fogies," or childish nuisances. They may be avoided, condescended to, or dealt with impatiently.

Once this scenario is in place, most of these folks tend

to respond in the ways they've grown accustomed to all their lives. When sons or daughters fail to phone regularly, they often adopt a blaming approach, designed to arouse guilt.

"I guess you're just too busy to find a few minutes for me. I could have had a stroke and died, for all you knew."

If grandchildren fail to find time for them, they complain to the parents, their own children. "I brought *you* up to respect your elders! What are you teaching *your* children, anyway?"

The result of such complaining and fault-finding is often arousal of resentment, guilt or defensiveness — as well as a growing desire for distance and detachment.

### *The Altroset Alternative*

It needn't be so. When people reach their middle and later years, they're especially good candidates for a lifestyle which is oriented *outward* rather than *inward*.

I call this lifestyle "Altroset." Since there is no single word for this outward style, I have coined "Altroset" from the Italian *altrui* (of or to others) and the educational term "set" (an established attitude). Using this word saves having to explain the idea each time it comes up.

Altroset is a combination of attitudes and behaviors which are intended to foster favorable responses from others without resort to blaming or faulting. An Altroset style can be a part of anyone's collection of relationship tools, at *any* age. However, it is particularly useful for older people, since it works to offset their tendency to be overly inward and overly sensitive.

Altroset describes a way of living which can be *deliberately learned and cultivated*.

Think about the many people you know. Some of them come across as primarily *self*-interested. You experience them as not really caring about you, not being truly aware of your needs, your preferences, your feelings. However, there are others who seem always to have their antennae out for what those around them are thinking and feeling. They seem to sense the meaning of what you say and do at a deeper level. They "understand" you.

The aim of Altroset is to extend your own antennae — to help you pick up signals from those around you, and thus to understand them better.

As a way of correcting those "golden age blues," Altroset reflects a caring attitude toward others, and often helps counteract the kind of self-involved preoccupation in later years that can alienate families and friends.

A healthy level of Altroset does not mean sacrificing oneself for the sake of others. It means *focusing* one's mental and emotional energies — consciously and deliberately — on what others are thinking and feeling.

Altroset is a major personal asset which tends to produce responsiveness in others, and helps pave the way for mutually gratifying feedback. In turn, this encourages feelings of security and self-esteem.

In short, Altroset is the self-serving road to selflessness.

Had Lester applied Altroset to his life, he might have avoided the preoccupation with frustration that left him wallowing in isolated self-pity.

People who deliberately tune in to the cues and signs of others and their needs (sometimes obvious, sometimes only implied), are inclined to forget about their own internal anxiety signals. They often gain a sense of competency and self-management that enables them to deal more comfortably with self-focussed concerns, such as their own aging, and the result can be a significant reduction in mental health problems and related psychosomatic symptoms, such as headaches and stomach distress.

Blame and fault-finding aren't needed to produce the responses we most want from others. Interest and concern for them can.

Consider what happened to Mike, a 64-year-old plumbing contractor, and his wife Sheila.

Their 22-year-old son, Joseph, left their close-knit family unit when he married Lisa, a girl from another state whom he'd met in college. They moved to her home town, where Joseph started a business of his own.

Hurt that Joseph wasn't going to join the family business, as they had planned for years, Mike showed his distress only to Sheila. He looked forward to the dutifully regular phone calls his son made each Saturday afternoon, but he fumed inwardly, and began to feel more stressed by a variety of aches and pains that had started to bother him.

After a few months, Joseph's calls began to grow more terse and uncommunicative. Mike interpreted this as further evidence of his son's turning away from the family, and his conversations with Joseph became increasingly cool and distant.

"It's like the kid hasn't got time for us any more — just for his wife and his business and his new friends," he said sadly to Sheila as they waited for Joseph's call one Saturday.

She looked up from a letter she was reading, and replied, "Maybe this has something to do with it."

It was a note from her cousin, who lived in the town to which Joseph had moved. One paragraph read, "Got a glimpse of Joey coming out of a restaurant last night. He was alone, and he looked terrible. He pretended he didn't see me, and hurried away."

When the phone rang, Mike was prepared. After the usual noncommittal exchanges, he asked, "How's Lisa getting along? She working or anything?" There was a perceptible pause: "Yeah — I guess ... sure, she's all right." Joseph's voice was low.

Mike picked up immediately on the pause and tone: "Joey! I get the feeling something's wrong. I don't want to pry, but — are you *really* okay?"

Mike heard his son catch his breath, then begin to cry. Then the story came out. Lisa had found the marriage unsatisfactory and had left him. Joseph's distress, and his preoccupation with his marital troubles, had caused business errors that were adding to his woes. He felt miserable, but didn't want his parents to know, and so had kept his calls short and uncommunicative. Only when Mike reached out, newly *sensitive to his needs,* was Joseph prompted to open up and respond.

### Understanding Human Needs

The Altroset approach works best when you focus your attention on what *other people* want out of life and why they do what they do. This increases your awareness of others and helps develop your openness toward them — hallmark of the Altroset way of living.

Abraham Maslow was one of a small group of pioneering psychologists who suggested that the best way to get a handle on what people want, and why they do what they do, is to understand their *needs*. Maslow proposed that human needs may be viewed in terms of their *priority* in one's life — an idea he presented in the form of a pyramid, with *survival* needs as the foundation (including hunger, thirst, avoidance of physical injury, and sex — for survival of our species). Once physical survival is insured, we begin to pursue our needs at the other levels: *security, love, esteem* and *personal fulfillment* (including beauty, goodness and wholeness). Rare and thrillingly ecstatic or "peak" experiences top the pyramid and beckon us to greater heights, for once we have felt them we are likely to seek them again.

Until the fundamental needs are satisfied, the upper-level needs have little chance to gain attention. The tragedy of too many lives is that they are spent almost entirely at the two lowest levels.

The following list shows some examples of specific *behaviors* associated with each level of needs:

***Survival*** – The healthy expression of survival needs includes such activities as physical exercise, restful sleep habits and avoidance of dangerous drugs, as well as the obviously necessary attention to nourishing food, drink and shelter. Survival needs may be ignored when a strong emotion — such as blind rage — impels someone to act without regard for life itself.

***Security*** – Security means avoiding threats to your well-being, and protecting yourself against danger. Security needs cause us to save enough money to avoid hardship, to keep our doors locked at night, and to stay out of fights with people a foot taller than ourselves.

***Love*** – We humans are capable of a broad range of caring feelings and behaviors. Although romantic love and sex are the topics most often mentioned in discussions of love, human love needs also include, among others, a child's attachment to mother and father. The latter need is so powerful that it may even cause a child to cling to an abusive parent from whom a brutal beating has just been received.

Love is the warmest expression of closeness and connectedness of which humans are capable, whether toward friends, relatives, or even strangers. The giving of love (unless unrequited) seems to be almost as gratifying as receiving it.

***Esteem*** – When you mention casually how well you are doing on the job or in school, you are seeking esteem. Young men who tell tall tales of sexual prowess to locker room buddies are seeking esteem. Most human achievements — beyond those undertaken for survival or security — are designed, at least in part, to evoke esteem from others.

A high evaluation from others fosters feelings of self-worth and emotional security. When others de-value us, it is much more difficult to maintain self-esteem.

***Personal Fulfillment*** – This need is sometimes called "self-actualization." It's harder to pinpoint than the other need levels. In fact, Maslow claimed that only a few people manage their lives in ways that satisfy this need. *When* you do, you feel that you are giving fullness and richness to your life, and using your potentials at or near their highest capacity.

An artist who spends life painting works that reflect

his deepest self is meeting the need for personal fulfillment.

When a chef transcends the mechanics of cooking-by-recipe, to reach a level of creativity in food preparation that reflects her very own style, she too may feel self-actualized.

To find constructive outlets for the richest and deepest parts of ourselves — that is personal fulfillment.

*Peak Experiences* – It may be that the need for a peak experience is not felt at all — until the experience has occurred. Then it may spark a desire to live more deeply and fully than ever before.

The cure of a lifelong disease at Lourdes may be such an experience... or a dream-vision like the one that produced Coleridge's mystical "Kubla Khan"... or the ecstatic experience of a religious conversion.

Peak experiences are rare extensions of personal fulfillment, in moments of creative or spiritual achievement which go far beyond the everyday, even for individuals who live at the level of personal fulfillment.

### P.S.: *On Discovering Needs*

Now, try the following self-teaching experiment: Think of someone you know really well. Focus on that person's *needs,* with Maslow's pyramid in mind. What seems to motivate that person's actions? Try to connect the person's *needs* with his or her actual *behavior.* On a sheet of paper write all the needs you can think of that motivate this individual. *Try to list at least ten.* Allow yourself to include needs which seem trivial as well as those which are fundamental. Note especially the needs that seem to make the person different from others, since this will make your understanding of this individual more meaningful.

For example, while almost everyone seems to have a need for safety, one person may have a need to seek unusual *risks*. Knowing this tells us a good deal about the person. (Perhaps he or she is really searching for *esteem*.) At the other end of the spectrum is the individual who seems to have a special need to *avoid* risks. Someone else may have a need to win esteem from others by stressing sexual attractiveness, and so on.

For each need you identify, jot down a word or two which represents an example of how your friend's *behavior* expresses that need. For instance, the risk-avoiding person may shun strenuous games, airplane travel, stock investments. The risk-seeking person may express it through questionable tax deductions, betting on the horses, or mountain climbing.

When you finish, look over your list. You'll know a great deal more about that person than you did before!

The final step in this exercise is an Altroset "action plan." Based on your new understanding of your friend's needs, write down several steps *you* can take to relate better to him or her. How can you show your insight and sensitivity? (e.g. "I can listen to her more, and talk less." "I can stop teasing him about putting his money in the mattress.")

Please try this exercise. Apply the process to several of your friends and loved ones. As you practice this increased understanding and sensitivity to their needs, you will have moved your Altroset skills several notches higher.

# 12

## NOR BLAME THYSELF

$S$hakespeare's plays often reveal profound psychological insights. In the fifth act of *Macbeth*, a doctor and a gentlewoman hide in the shadows, observing Lady Macbeth as she walks in her sleep. She begins to rub her hands, as though washing them, more and more vigorously. The doctor questions his companion, "What does she now?" The gentlewoman responds that Lady Macbeth frequently performs this ritual.

Suddenly, we hear Lady Macbeth speak. "Yet here's a spot," she says, still rubbing her spotless hands. "Out, damned spot! Out, I say!... What, will these hands ne'er be clean?"

The audience is watching a classic example of a compulsive ritual, used — futilely — to wash away nagging, merciless guilt. Earlier in the play, Lady Macbeth had incited her husband to murder, and now her conscience is exacting a toll. Suffering from a critical case of self-blame, she repeatedly attempts to wipe invisible blood stains from her hands.

More than guilt, it is the accompanying self-punishment that concerns us here. Everyone experiences guilt, and, uncomfortable though it is, it often serves useful social purposes. It can, for example, deter us from acting in ways that might harm others. But it is also widely and harmfully misused. Children's guilt tendencies are strengthened by their parents, who often resort to playing on them as a means of maintaining control.

### Guilty As Charged

Most of us can recall times when we were blamed and made to feel guilty. One result of such experiences is that we learned to blame ourselves, sometimes to excess.

When Marty was four, his harassed mother's most frequently used words to her sensitive and highly active son were, "Stop doing that!" and "No, no, no! Why are you such a *bad boy?*" Invariably, he would cry out, "I'm *not* a bad boy!" Then he would burst into tears.

By the time he was twelve, his mother's message had "grown-up." Now it was, "You're *always* getting into trouble! What's the matter with you?" He no longer cried or answered back — for if he did, he was accused of being the "most disrespectful boy in the world!" Instead, he would bolt from the house, wordlessly.

By sixteen, Marty was almost as convinced as his

parents that he was responsible for making their life a "hell on earth."

When he was eighteen, he had his first serious relationship with a girl. When she claimed he had made her pregnant, they were married within a month. Marty was convinced he was responsible, in spite of his friends' insistence that she had been sexually involved with at least three other young men during that time. But Marty wasn't answering to reason, only to guilt.

The baby miscarried, and Marty also managed to blame himself for that — contending that he must have taken inadequate care of his wife. When she divorced him less than a year later, he was immersed again in a sea of shame and self-blame — although his friends swore she'd been extending favors to other men for most of the brief marriage.

Like Lady Macbeth, Marty was unable to cleanse the non-existent blood from his hands even though, unlike her, he bore none of the actual blame.

One explanation for this guilt-acceptance was theorized by Sigmund Freud. He believed that imposition of blame by parents becomes part of a person's self-perception, buried in a section of the psyche which he called the *superego*. Once blame and guilt have been internalized in this way, according to Freud, the person continues to do the blaming — and to induce self-guilt — even when the parents are not present (even long after they have died).

Whether produced directly by parents, as happened with Marty, or by the superego (an internalized substitute for parents), as with Lady Macbeth, self-imposed guilt is frequently harmful to one's ability to function effectively.

Just like external blame, internal guilt diminishes self-esteem, impairs self-confidence, and causes withdrawal into oneself and/or construction of neurotic mechanisms to defend against the pain.

### *To Err Is Human...*

Just as I have urged you not to blame others, because of the chilling, alienating effect it has on them, and on your relationships with them, so I am also urging that you not blame yourself, and for the very same reasons. Take responsibility, yes! Make whatever changes are necessary to correct errors, yes! But don't beat yourself with blame and guilt because you've made a mistake. Do what you can about it, honestly, and then move on!

If your motives were good and, for any number of reasons, the results were not, it makes no sense to blame yourself. If you erred because you were careless, blaming yourself serves no purpose except, perhaps, to make you feel worse. Then you can let yourself off the hook by rationalizing how much you're "suffering" for your mistake.

The no-blame philosophy encourages self-growth in both you and the significant people in your life, no matter how close or how casual the relationship. Such self-growth cannot fail to enhance your relationships by increasing the openness and warmth of your communication.

When you avoid blaming others you allow them to feel comfortable and secure with you. When you avoid blaming *yourself*, you accomplish exactly the same thing. Accept yourself. Create an inner environment that allows you to correct things that need correcting, while insuring freedom to grow in confidence and security.

Here are some practical suggestions, including "SELF-STATEMENTS" to use as helpful reminders of what's really important:

• *Be clear about your intentions.*
If you act in good faith, and something goes wrong, you are *not* to blame.

Five-year-old Becky is a small but revealing example. When her mother asked her to help unload a shopping bag by carrying a bottle of fruit juice to the refrigerator, she tried to be very careful, but the bottle was wet, slipped out of her hands, and smashed on the floor.

Becky cried and cried, sobbing over and over, "I'm sorry! I'm a bad girl! I'm sorry! I'm a bad girl!" She was the unfortunate product of a mothering style that emphasized blame and guilt in child-training.

However, her mother had been re-learning her role in a parenting group. She stopped everything she was doing, put her arms around her child and said, "Honey, you're *not* a bad girl. You tried to do it right. Anyone can make a mistake."

What Becky's mother gave to her, and what you need to give to yourself in equivalent situations, was the SELF-STATEMENT:
*I honestly tried to do it right.*

• *You can make a mistake and still be a good person.*
Becky's mother made that clear to her, and you can keep it clear in your own mind, with the SELF-STATEMENT:
*I've tried my best, so there's no need to feel guilty.*

• *Do whatever you can to remedy the hurtful conse-quences of your actions.*

No matter how good your intentions, you should do everything possible to correct what has gone wrong, if what you did was harmful in any way. Only through making that effort can you fully clear away the pain or distress attached to what happened.

Becky's mother cleaned up the dangerous pieces of glass from the broken bottle, then set her to work mopping up the juice. Finished at last, Becky looked up with a bright, triumphant smile, and said, "All fixed!" She felt herself a worthwhile person once more. For your own use, here is an important SELF- STATEMENT:

*No matter what my intentions, if I have hurt someone, I'll try to fix it or make amends.*

• *It serves no purpose whatever to lay blame or guilt on yourself, once you have done everything in your power to remedy a hurt you may have caused.*

When this is clear, you can focus on the appropriate final SELF- STATEMENT;

*I take responsibility for my actions — not guilt!*

# 13

## MASKING, MANEUVERING, MANIPULATING

*D*estructive guilt-inducing blame may lurk behind a friend's most "innocent" advice: "Well, I think you're foolish if you...." A spouse's most "sincere" constructive criticism may actually disguise a hostile put-down: "I'm sure you could get a raise, if only you'd...." More often than you might think, blaming and faulting are neatly hidden behind deceptive words and ideas. When this happens, their target may have difficulty detecting the ill-will involved.

Language is charged with many meanings and nuances. Words call up associations from memory, to give them richness, subtlety and special meaning. Tone of voice, gestures, facial expressions, posture, and circumstances all have the power to alter the quality of the same words and phrases.

The intent behind words is a crucial factor. The same expression may be used to hurt or heal. Let's take a look at ways to identify intent, apart from the words themselves.

### Politics Can Turn Friends Into Strangers

Vinnie and Ray had been friends for many years in spite of the fact that they hold sharply differing political views. Vinnie had been smarting ever since Ray's choice won the presidency and, in Vinnie's view, had been ruining the country ever since.

One evening they were discussing the current race for the office, debating the merits of the contending candidates. As the conversation warmed up, Vinnie grew more frustrated with his friend's stubborn dissent. Interrupting Ray in mid-sentence, he said earnestly, "If people like you hadn't voted for that guy in the White House last time, we could have avoided the mess we're in now! I know, I know, you honestly believed you were right. But isn't it about time to admit you made a mistake, and vote sensibly this time — not on the basis of impressions or emotions?"

"*You* say we're in a mess," Ray said, in a predictable response. "*I* say we're doing fine." He then launched into a heated defense of his vote and listed what he thought were the administration's successes.

The conversation never did get around to an objective analysis of the new candidates.

Vinnie didn't put-down his friend directly. Instead, he used carefully chosen words — such as "people like you" — to imply Ray's inferior status. But the effect of his words was the same: they produced resentment and defensiveness.

The phrase, "admit you made a mistake," is another indirect blaming phrase, as is Vinnie's accusation that Ray's vote was based on "impressions and emotions."

Vinnie managed to blame Ray without ever having to point his finger directly at him. His disclaimer, "I know, I know, you honestly believed you were right," is a common *mask* for finding fault and blaming. Ray's reaction was to respond to the *blaming,* not the issues or opinions behind them. He felt defensive, and unwilling to accept Vinnie's arguments, valid or not. His energies were focused on warding off blame.

Politics is a volatile subject. Still, Vinnie and Ray could have entered into a thoughtful discussion without blaming and assessing fault, masked or direct.

Like most people, Vinnie was uncomfortable when charged with using blame tactics, so he disguised them. Such masking rarely succeeds.

### Don't Shout Over Spilt Milk

Another example of "masking" involved Lloyd, a twenty-three-year-old newlywed who had never developed routine shopping skills. One day, after Lloyd had gone to the store for milk, his wife opened the refrigerator and found milk dripping from all three shelves and pooling at the bottom. Phyllis exclaimed in dismay, "What *happened?*"

She quickly discovered the problem — a crack in the bottom of the milk carton. She cleaned the mess, then turned to Lloyd and asked harshly, "Didn't you *know* there was a crack in the container?" Her real message, in essence: "How could you be so dumb?" Or, perhaps, "If you did know it, and put the carton in there anyway, you're even *dumber*!"

"Of course I didn't know!" came his indignant reply. "Are you nuts? Why would I intentionally put a leaking carton in the refrigerator?"

Lloyd was responding to the *intent* behind Phyllis' words — blame. He was answering the unstated message that he was guilty — if not of carelessness, then of sheer stupidity.

The ill-feelings passed soon enough, but the exchange reflected a way of communicating that would continue to trouble Lloyd and Phyllis in the future.

In a productive, blame-avoiding relationship, it is *assumed* that the other person's intentions are good. And, if the intentions are good, blame is not appropriate. If intentions are *not* seen as good, a much deeper problem exists, one that could be seriously destructive to the marriage. If it cannot be satisfactorily resolved, the question becomes: Is the relationship worth keeping?

Masked blaming and faulting can take many forms. Probably the best known is, "I told you so!" Variants include, "I warned you not to do that!" and "I told you you'd get into trouble!" They all say, in essence, "You're to be *blamed* for not listening to me, because I'm smarter (or better) than you."

A more subtle phrase, frequently used on children, is: "Wait till you're older. Then you'll understand!" That is: "You're just too stupid and immature to see how right I am."

Sometimes this manipulative mask has a more general application, not limited to children: "If you had more knowledge of what I'm talking about, you'd see that I'm right." The implication is, of course, that the other person is ignorant.

Perhaps the most transparent mask of all is the statement that often prefaces a criticism: "I don't want to tell you this, but I have to, *for your own sake...*" Or the classic variant: "I'm only telling you this *for your own good!*"

### Unmasking Blame

How can you know when blame is really lurking behind a mask, maneuver or manipulation? How can you measure the sincerity of expressions of surprise or hurt at the mere suggestion that blaming or faulting was intended?

Very simple: Do the words make you feel guilty, or lower your self-esteem? Do they make you feel defensive or belittled?

If so, you've been blamed.

It's the same if you get a sense that the remarks are intended to make the other person feel superior.

If you *feel* slighted, even though you have trouble identifying the slight among the "kind" masking words — you've *been* slighted!

### Watch Out for These Cues

Following are several guidelines that can help alert you to blaming or faulting hidden behind an innocent-seeming communication. None of them should be taken as automatic cause to reject what's being said to you. But you're entitled to think twice about the intent of the speaker when you're alerted by them. If you have additional guidelines of your own that you find useful in recognizing hidden putdowns, by all means add them to the list. (And don't forget to apply these same guidelines as warning signs when *you* may be about to use a masked putdown on someone else!):

• Statements that begin with apparent praise or approval, followed by "but" or "except." If what comes next is blame or fault-finding, the first part is irrelevant.

Example: "You know how much I admire your intelligence, but you really didn't use it in this instance, did you?"

Example: "I love the way you did your hair today — it's too bad the color was such a bad choice." (Here the word "except" is left out, but it's clearly understood, after the first part of the sentence.)

• Statements that start with assurances of only the best intentions — and finish on a note of blame or fault. Again, the first part is irrelevant if what follows is hurtful.

Example: "You know I'm always concerned about you, and how you're feeling. When you came in wearing that outfit yesterday, I thought you no longer gave a damn how you look!"

• Statements that assign you to a category of people considered in some way unworthy or unacceptable — without explicitly tarring you with the same brush.

Example: "I know what you said is what all the *radical* groups believe, but I take a different position!" (This, of course, makes use of the tactic of guilt by association.)

• Statements that disclaim the speaker's knowledge or expertise, but offer an unfavorable judgment nevertheless.

Example: "I'm not an expert on psychotherapy, but you certainly seem more easily upset these days than when you started treatment."

• Statements that "tack on" criticism to a high-principled positive comment.

Example: "I certainly believe in the principle that everyone is entitled to an opinion, even when it's just plain pigheaded and wrong!"

• Statements that use the word "even" as a lead-in to an *assumption* which disguises blaming or faulting.

Example: "Even Herbie passed that exam, didn't he? I guess all the *good* students got A's."

You felt pleased at getting a B+ on that exam, until that was said to you. Since Herbie is known to be a poor student, the *assumption* the speaker made (and used against you) was that unless you got an A it was no great achievement.

In all of these examples, it's hard to charge the speaker with intention to find fault with you. But it takes only a little thought — and a little attention to your gut feelings — to make you aware that you've been put down.

The remedy? When it's done to you, tell the other person openly how you feel, and discuss what can be done about it. When you're the one doing it — or about to do it — to someone else, *don't!*

Even behind a mask, blaming is blaming. And it's not healthy.

# 14

## So What Do You Do About It?

*B*y this point in the book, you may be thinking, "Okay, if it's so socially destructive and self-defeating to seek to influence people through finding fault and blaming, how do I influence people *constructively?* How can I bring about changes I consider necessary?

No-fault living does *not* mean acceptance of the unacceptable. Everyone needs to influence others at times — to insure safety and security, to achieve goals, to bring pleasure to our lives. Children need to be taught desirable patterns of behavior, along with social survival skills. Family members and friends need to be urged to alter offensive behaviors.

How do we employ the philosophy of no-fault to bring about these changes?

Most people already use some effective methods of bringing about change in others, but in haphazard ways. Some techniques are less familiar. You're most effective when you employ all the methods in a planned and systematic fashion, rather than randomly or impulsively.

### Does Might Really Make Right?

The oldest and most primitive method of "influencing" people is the use of superior force — applied by one with greater power to bring about change in a weaker person. When used by parents to control children, the assumption is that it's necessary in order to teach them discipline and respect. Unfortunately, force used this way often results in fear and pain, and so teaches that, first and foremost, hurting others is the most effective way to achieve goals.

Imposing pain, physical *or* mental (as in blaming and faulting) often does produce results — *temporarily*. But it also produces resentment and hostility. And it's only effective when the source of pain (e.g. the parent) is present.

### "Grandma Knows Best"

There are two other more civilized and lastingly effective approaches to influencing the behavior of others. The first is "The Law of Consequences." In educational circles, with a bit of whimsy, it is also called "Grandma's Law."

Eight-year-old Johnny is visiting Grandma. Since the visit first was planned, he has been looking forward to one of Grandma's home-baked apple pies. So, when he sits down to his dinner of meat, potatoes and spinach, he really is thinking of the freshly-baked pie resting on the counter.

Johnny gobbles down the meat and potatoes, eyeing the pie the whole while. But he balks at the spinach. He hates spinach. He knows that, at home, if he raises enough of a ruckus, he usually can get out of eating it.

Grandma, however, doesn't play by those rules. She responds with a benign smile when he makes a face at the spinach. "Eat the spinach, Johnny," she says simply. "You'll get a piece of pie as soon as you're finished."

"But..."

"No spinach, no pie. Grandma's Law."

His protests are ignored. Johnny eats the spinach and gets the pie.

Grandma might put it this way: "First you do what *I* want you to do, then you can do what *you* want to do."

According to the Law of Consequences, an act followed by an unpleasant consequence tends not to be repeated. When the consequence is pleasant, the action tends to be encouraged. If this happens *regularly* and *consistently,* it has a permanent effect on the behavior pattern.

Two things make this law particularly effective. It gives notice of the consequences to follow an act, and the consequence is directly associated with the act. Whenever possible, the consequences should follow immediately. Had Johnny not eaten his spinach, the consequence would have been no pie.

While it's true that spanking (force) is also an unpleasant consequence, it has at least three drawbacks: it connects learning with pain (and in that sense is counterproductive); it is only effective while the spanker (parent) is present to inflict the punishment (and thus does not teach self-discipline); and it teaches violence as an appropriate way to behave (and we know that those who grow up with violence tend to employ violence as adults).

Earlier, we described another example of the Law of Consequences. You may recall, in Chapter Four, Doris warned her husband, Ben, that he would be denied the pleasures of sex if he continued to make the act painful for her. She "played fair" by giving him warning, and connecting his actions with the consequences that would result. It was his choice.

The major drawback to unpleasant consequences is that they only *deter* behavior. They don't cause *preferred* behaviors to occur. To bring about preferred behavior patterns, we must examine the "flip side" of the Law of Consequences. That is, *favorable consequences tend to encourage behavior you desire.*

The apple pie was a favorable consequence for Johnny. If Grandma also had made a point of rewarding Johnny's eating the spinach by praising him, it would have made a stronger impression. Praise is a pleasurable consequence on its own. Often it's the most effective consequence of all.

Over-all, I believe that favorable consequences should outnumber unfavorable ones at least three to one. It is true that some people respond well to material consequences, such as gifts, sex, money or apple pie. However, long-term changes in behavior tend more to be the result of sincere praise as an immediate consequence of desired behavior.

Praise, when sincerely given, encourages feelings of security and confidence. Even more, it involves some of the feelings connected with its not-so-distant cousin, love.

More than the need to be praised, the need to be loved seems to be a universal human condition. After basic survival, love may be the most fundamental of motivating forces in human behavior; and it's a force that does not diminish one whit with advanced age. However, if love is offered as a *condition* for a particular behavior, one may doubt its sincerity and dependability.

Affection is a less intense aspect of love which can be a highly effective way of influencing behavior.

Praise and affection are consequences given and withheld almost automatically when relating to children. Yet adults are fully as responsive to them as any child. People tend to give praise and affection impulsively on occasion, but only infrequently is it employed as a method of deliberately influencing behavior. I encourage you to pay more attention to the intentional use of praise and affection in your everyday relationships.

The Law of Consequences is highly effective when applied methodically. Changing behavior in a relationship should be based on a consistent and honest strategy. Tell 'em what you're going to do, then *do* it!

### *"Now That Makes Sense!"*

There is a second major approach to influencing behavior: the "Make-sense" strategy. Like praise and affection, it often is used in random ways, without explicit recognition of its power to influence people.

Imagine you are working on a complicated jigsaw puzzle, say the picture of a city harbor at evening. You are piecing together a section that seems particularly difficult. The golden sunset has all its pieces *satisfyingly* in place. But a boat that is supposed to be floating on the gentle waters is missing. The fragments of that boat lie somewhere among the loose pieces scattered on the table.

As you finger the loose pieces and move them around on the table, the form of the sailboat starts to appear. Then the pieces begin to fit into the curves of the already existing puzzle, and — aha! you've got it! Now everything seems to fall into place. The feeling of satisfaction returns, more strongly than before.

The "aha!" experience when something fits is the key to the make-sense approach to changing behavior patterns.

Studies in Gestalt psychology have shown that the human nervous system feels a lessening of tension and a sense of satisfaction when things "fit," in whatever way the situation calls for.

An unfinished jigsaw puzzle offers a challenge. As more and more pieces fit together, there is a growing sense of achievement — you're making progress toward a solution. *Full* satisfaction, however, comes to you only when *all* the pieces fit.

When we try to solve problems in daily life, we move ideas and memories around in our minds, until — "aha!" — they fit, like jigsaw pieces. The tension of the unsolved problem is relieved. *The result makes sense.*

This feeling seems to demand that we act in accordance with the logic. As some of our greatest thinkers have pointed out, the need to make sense of the world around us is a constant force in life.

How does this fit in with the picture of human interaction that we've been constructing? *If I am convinced that what you are telling me makes sense, that it "fits" with my own understanding of what's appropriate, then I have a hard time acting in opposition to it.*

Seventeen-year-old Bobby and his mother provide a case in point. Having spent an evening with friends, Bobby came home after his parents had gone to bed. In the morning, his mother, up early, went outside for the newspaper. She noticed that Bobby had failed to double-lock the front door.

When he came downstairs she could have been angry: "How come you forgot to lock the door last night again? Can't you ever remember anything?"

However, Bobby's mother chose a different tack, a make-sense approach. When Bobby came downstairs, she looked up from the newspaper. "Some more burglaries in our neighborhood," she said. "It's frightening. Did you know the Rands' house down the block was broken into last month? They had a cheap safety lock — easy to break open. They heard someone. Mr. Rand came downstairs and the burglar threatened to kill him! I would have died of *fright*!

"Please, Bobby, try not to forget the safety lock. We have a *good* one. But it's only good if it gets used!"

This approach made it easy for Bobby to promise to be more conscientious in the future, rather than react negatively and defensively.

His mother had provided him with two strong, effective, sensible reasons: if he neglects the lock, he makes the family, and himself, vulnerable to a real danger; moreover, he worries his mother. These considerations make sense to him.

The effect of the Law of Consequences could have been added to the "make-sense" approach. Bobby's mother could have continued with, "This is really important to me, so I'm going to make a new policy. Each time you forget to lock up you'll be grounded for a Saturday night." (Note that the *consequence* of misbehavior — staying home — is directly related to the *source* of the problem — going out.)

Both the Law of Consequences and the Make-sense approach work best when they are used with full awareness of the other person's needs and thought processes. Proposing a consequence that doesn't meaningfully affect the person is unlikely to produce results. In this regard, Altroset, which we discussed in Chapter Eleven, makes a strong contribution by stressing  awareness of others' feelings and views.

### Attention and Praise:
#### The Most Powerful Consequences

Often awareness of someone's attitudes or needs will affect your efforts to change a behavior. For instance, a child who receives very little parental attention may increase undesirable behavior when spoken to harshly. Even a stern comment is bringing the child attention, something badly needed and sought. Even adults who crave attention sometimes behave annoyingly, in order to get noticed — regardless of the unpleasantness of the actual response.

For such people, a more effective method might be to provide attention only in response to behavior that is in any way *desirable.*  In this way, he or she receives the desperately wanted attention while learning appropriate behaviors to gain it.

An example of adult behavior modified with praise comes from Loretta's husband, Ira. Their friends call him

"Impatient Ike," because of his short temper and irritability when he has to wait for anything.

On one occasion he drove his wife to the supermarket and waited for her outside. Loretta was upset when the marketing took longer than expected. She was sure she would be hit with a tirade when she returned to the car. Instead, because it was a nice day and he was in an unusually good mood, Ike simply greeted her with a smile and an amiable comment.

She immediately took the opportunity to comment, "You know, honey, you really are more patient than people give you credit for. I feel great that you're not angry with me about having to wait."

Her appreciation, which is a particularly effective form of praise, coupled with her compliment, moved Ike in the direction of greater patience on other occasions as well.

### *Three's Company... A Fourth Can Help*

Professional counseling also can provide much needed help. The following instance demonstrates how various methods work together in a real-life situation.

Lila is twenty-four years old, tall, strikingly pretty and quite shy. Because of her shyness, she has tied herself into a dependent friendship with a married couple in their early thirties, Tina and Mort.

Mort, without acknowledging any special interest, developed a particularly possessive "big brother" attitude toward Lila. This was most apparent whenever they discussed her dating relationships. Mort was quick to lecture her on how she should behave with her male friends, and became angry if she disagreed with his admonitions.

Because of his own insecurities, Mort wanted both

women to acknowledge his intellectual "superiority," and took offense at any indication that Lila or Tina might be just as intelligent as he. In addition, he felt threatened by the fact that Lila's earnings as a dental hygienist were comparable to his. (Tina was not employed outside their home.)

Despite Mort's intrusiveness, Lila enjoyed the security that the friendship brought her, and her relationship with Tina had grown strong. After one particularly heated argument with Mort, Lila's distress over the direction the friendship was taking led her to discuss the situation with a counselor.

The counselor helped Lila to decide that she would tell Mort she recognized and appreciated his concern for her, but she needed *him* to recognize that the *manner* with which he expressed it made her feel pressured and beaten down.

With support from the counselor, Lila concluded that she would simply not stay around any time Mort's "lectures" made her uncomfortable. He would have to stop his badgering or she would quietly leave, rather than be upset.

Acting on the plan, Lila made her feelings and intentions known to Mort and Tina, without blaming or faulting Mort. Then she waited. On two occasions after that, Mort's admonishments became intolerable. Each time, she stood up, said good-night, and left — to the considerable consternation of the other two.

It worked. She successfully applied the Law of Consequences in direct response to the stated problem. Her "make-sense" warning helped Mort and Tina understand what was happening..

The outcome was a major change in the relationship. Lila was able to keep the positive aspects of the friendship, while modifying the negative ones and, in addition, she felt a significant increase in her own sense of self-esteem and confidence. She had taken charge of a damaging aspect of a relationship and changed it. There had been no anger, no shouting, no blaming and no putdowns — none of the destructive measures that spoil relationships and hinder growth.

# 15

## *Putting It All Together*

*T*here is a real need for all of us to re-examine the ways in which we deal with one another. Lost friendships, damaged business connections, and hurt loved ones are just a few of the unfortunate results when we magnify the deficits of others and the inconveniences they cause. Blaming and fault-finding have harmful effects for everyone involved.

The story of Jody is an example of the kind of long-term injury that unhealthy criticism can cause.

A soft-mannered, twenty-two-year old only a year out of college, Jody sought help because she was developing severe insomnia that was already ruining her career. She was so worried about the demands of her career, and so fearful of making mistakes, that she lay awake most nights agonizing over the next day's activities. She had already been fired for inattention at her first job as a business trainee, and was in danger of being fired from her second for the same reason.

Exhausted after each night's bout with anxiety and sleeplessness, she simply lacked the stamina to concentrate effectively at work.

Sleeping pills helped temporarily, but soon lost their effectiveness. Tranquilizers seemed to make little difference. Even a night in a sleep clinic, wired to recording instruments, provided no solution.

Jody came to counseling desperate and in tears. Exploring her history, she spoke of caring but financially harassed parents who had impressed on her the importance of career success. Though only slightly above average in intelligence, she had done well in college by virtue of a perfectionistic drive and long hours of study.

Exploring her history further, the heart of her problem became apparent: At every turn in her childhood, Jody was judged by her loving but demanding and perpetually critical mother — and too often found lacking. Finding fault and assessing blame were Mama's response to every small mistake.

As a result, Jody grew up filled with self-doubt and guilt, wanting desperately to please, increasingly anxious to avoid making a mistake. Her perfectionistic style worked for her in school and college, but it was a liability when she faced the unaccustomed pressures of the business world.

Every night, she left notes around her room to remind her of assignments to be done the following day — even though she never forgot even the smallest of them. In spite of the notes, she lay awake at night, terrified that she might forget or perform a task incorrectly.

Jody's lack of self-confidence and high anxiety were the results, at least in part, of the critical, blaming, fault-finding pressures from her mother, however loving the feeling behind them.

Jody's was an extreme problem that required years of counseling to correct. But similar effects occur, even though usually to a lesser degree, whenever blame and fault play a significant part in human relations.

So why do we do it? If constant criticism is so damaging, why do parents, teachers, bosses and others use it so often? If Jody's mom really loved her, why was she continually finding fault?

It does seem strange that blaming and faulting play such a large part in even the most loving relationships, in view of the damage they do. But they have been so deeply imbedded in our culture, for such a long time, that most people assume this is the proper, natural way to bring about changes in others.

Much of the problem has to do with how difficult it is to keep perspective. Most folks find it very hard to differentiate between large violations and small missteps.

One woman burst into a tirade when her husband failed to telephone that he would be late from work. Her outburst was so vitriolic that it might have been directed toward someone who had committed a heinous crime. She

even ended with a serious suggestion that they divorce.
While their history together explained part of her
reaction, it still far exceeded an appropriate response to
the specific event.

### The "Intensity Index"
### — A Tool To Help Reduce Blaming and Faulting

Development of a sense of proportion is an important
step toward avoiding hurtful fault/blame relationships. A
tool that I've labeled the "Intensity Index" can be of help
to almost anyone, and has worked well for a number of my
clients who have tried it as part of their experience in
counseling.

To begin, establish your standard with a scale of 1–10.
Imagine that the person you love most in the world has
been hit by a car and taken to the hospital, with life
hanging by a thread. Give the strength of your feelings
about this an Intensity Index number of 10, the highest
value on your scale.

Next, ask yourself what your feelings would be if a
not-very-close neighbor lay in the hospital suffering the
same misfortune. Would the Index number for those feelings be a 4, perhaps, or less?

Now, what number would you give to your feelings
about a badly cooked steak in a restaurant? Maybe a 2? (I
have seen people react as though it were a 15!)

Practice with the Intensity Index. Apply it to actual
events. Let it sharpen your judgment and correct your
sense of proportion. More and more, blaming and fault-
finding will be seen as inappropriate, as high-numbered,
intensely felt provocations become fewer.

As soon as you begin to draw back from destructive

ways of relating, you begin to create a new atmosphere for every relationship.

Lifelong habits are embedded and hard to give up, even those that can be as damaging as blaming and faulting. But picture for a moment what your present loves, friendships and associations would be like if warmth and acceptance replaced belittlement, criticism and guilt. It can happen!

Even a moderate reduction in the old ways can make a substantial change. The difference experienced by those who have given it a sincere try is significant and rewarding. Tensions are lowered, and cooperative efforts increased.

Does giving up your blaming and faulting habit seem too radical a change? Here's a suggestion: Resolve to refrain, consciously and deliberately, from assessing blame or fault for *one day*... then *two days*... then *a week*. After the week is up, talk to the important people in your life about how you felt doing this. Ask them if they noticed a difference in you. Ask them how *they* felt.

Discuss the difficulties you had in managing the no-fault lifestyle, and how they were — or could have been —resolved. Let the experience prove the net worth of the effort.

### *A Few Final — Crucial — Thoughts*

Most people assume that their needs and beliefs are right and good, and that their expectations of others are also right and good. It follows that if they are right, those who oppose them must necessarily be wrong. So blaming and finding fault are "appropriate" responses.

When we put it that bluntly, it's hard to miss the error

in the logic. It would be strange indeed for your thinking always to be right, and the other person's always wrong. In fact, other people's beliefs are just as valid to them as yours are to you.

In the absence of willful wrongdoing, faulting and blaming cannot be justified at all.

We all have the right to make our needs clear, and to seek to have others satisfy those needs in ways not harmful to themselves. What I have been saying throughout this book is that the methods most folks have used are counter-productive.

If the needs of others do not mesh with yours, you could choose to modify your desires occasionally for the sake of the relationship. This sometimes produces the most satisfying outcome of all, since there is deep gratification in arriving at harmony with others through change in oneself.

On the other hand, if your feelings of discontent with a relationship remain profound and unchangeable, and the other person cannot or will not take steps needed to make it work, abandoning that relationship does not mean failure or catastrophe. It might mean only that the destructive forces inherent in that particular association could not be overcome, even after sincere and honest effort.

The question might come up: Aren't the changes urged in this book just a matter of semantics? Of using "nice" words instead of "bad" ones? Far from it! The *attitude* behind the words is as important as the words themselves. So long as you assume that blaming and finding fault are natural and appropriate ways to influence others, this assumption will come through no matter what words you use. And since words are used to express both thoughts and feelings, the harmful intent will come through, as well.

I hope that I have persuaded you just how destructive it is to blame and fault, and how magically nurturant it can be to human relationships if we drop those habits from our lives. The "right words" — without fault or blame — won't come automatically however. You'll need to work hard in order to avoid blaming, finding fault, putting down and laying on guilt. Practice non-blaming phrases, such as, "I think that would work better if you did it the other way," instead of, "It was *stupid* of you not to see you were doing it wrong!" Try "It bothered me when you hung up on me," instead of, "You're a hateful, inconsiderate person for hanging up like that!"

It is also important to note that avoiding blame and fault- finding may have a direct effect on your *physical*, as well as your emotional, well-being.

The evidence is growing that hostile people tend to develop more physical illnesses than people who act kindly and are concerned about the welfare of others. When you shun blame and fault, you permit the caring part of yourself to emerge and find expression. Not only do you then benefit others; you benefit yourself.

With the No-Fault philosophy in place in your life, most relationships grow closer and warmer.

The goals of No-Fault Living are simple but not easy to achieve: a lifestyle that can provide warm, loving relationships in all parts of your life; to help *others* grow and enjoy life; and to bring you more emotional rewards than you might get through any other means.

It's a powerful *new* way to win friends, influence people, and make daily living really worthwhile — and it's available to you right now!

To help you make this a part of your everyday life, Chapter Sixteen offers ten "Magic Guidelines" for No-Fault Living...

# THE "MAGIC 10" GUIDELINES FOR SUCCESSFUL NO-FAULT LIVING

1. *Don't blame* the other person for behaviors you find objectionable. (Blaming causes guilt, shame, resentment and emotional withdrawal.)

2. *Don't fault* the other person just because of words or deeds that don't fit into patterns and expectations in your own mind. (Faulting produces defensiveness, retaliation or emotional distance.)

3. *Do express* your own feelings and accept responsibility for them (*"I'm mad* at you for what you did..."* instead of *"You made* me mad...").

4. *Do ask* others to *change* behaviors that hurt or upset you, or that you deem important to have changed for their sake.

5. *Do explain* why you want a change, so that your request *makes sense (compellingly logical sense) to that person.*

6. *Do set clear consequences* for acts of others: pleasurable consequences for desired actions, unpleasant consequences for objectionable ones. (Keep unpleasant consequences *minimal* at the beginning, increasing their severity slowly and only if truly necessary.)

7. *Do recognize* that others may see certain behaviors as right, even when you see them as wrong. Try to clarify the real meaning and purpose behind what you want and what others want. You all have an equal right to an opinion!

8. *Do compromise* if you can, for the sake of the relationship, if you don't have to yield on a strongly held principle.

9. *When in doubt, try the Intensity Index.* It will help you recognize how important — or *unimportant* — a disturbing event really is.

10. Never forget to ask yourself the crucial "Outcome" question: Putting aside my immediate feelings, *will what I do or say now help or hurt the relationship?*

*ALL* RELATIONSHIPS WORK BETTER WHEN *NOBODY* BLAMES *ANYBODY* FOR *ANYTHING.*

## Postscript

The following verse expresses the essence of the views presented in this book. As poetry, I fear it is, as Shakespeare put it, "An ill-favored thing, sire, but mine own." In any case, I am deeply convinced of its universal value in the realm of human relationships.

*I'll always remember*
*That some time, somewhere,*
*When it comes to mistakes*
*I've made my full share.*

*So for all the world's gold,*
*And for all the world's pelf,*
*I will not blame anyone —*
*Not even myself!*

GA

## *Post-Postscript*

To re-phrase the biblical admonition:

> *Let whoever is without fault*
> *cast the first stone.*

# INDEX

Acceptance, 11, 52, 54, 58
   non-judgmental, 36
Adler, Alfred, 43
Adolescence, 7, 44, 53
Affection, 109
Aging, 77-82
Altroset, 82-83, 85, 89, 112
Anger, 11, 63, 66, 111, 113, 115
Anxiety, 70, 73, 80-81, 118-119
Approval, 102
Assumption, 3, 100, 122-123
Attention, 112
Attitude, 82, 112, 122

Being "right," 9
Belittlement, 11, 101, 121
Blaming/Faulting effect, 41
"Bottom-line self-quiz," 33-34
Business, 69-75

Children, 35-37, 49, 52, 54-57, 106,
   112
Communication(s), 38, 64, 94, 101
Consequences, 20, 56, 57, 107-109,
   112, 126
   Law of, 106-109, 111-112, 114
Criticism, 38, 63, 65-66, 97, 101, 103,
   118-119, 121
Culture, 10, 119

Defensiveness, 82, 99, 101, 125
Divorce, 15, 32
   no-fault, 6

Employees, 70, 75
Expectations, 50, 78

Force, 106, 107-108
Freud, Sigmund, 10, 40, 93
Friend(s), 59-60
Friendship(s), 66, 68, 113-115

Gestalt, 110
"Golden Dozen"
   (marital partner qualities), 28, 31
Grandma's Law, 106-107
Guilt, 39-40, 82, 92-94, 121
Gut feelings, 103

Hostility, 97, 106
Human needs, 52, 86-89

Inferiority, 43, 45
Influence, 10, 105-106, 109
Insecurities, 45, 77
Intensity Index, 120, 126
Intentions, 95, 96, 98, 100, 101-102,
   114
Intimacy, 60, 68

Life style, 121, 123
Love, 87, 108-109
Lovers, 59-60

Macbeth, 91-92, 93
"Magic 10" Guidelines, 125-126
Make-sense strategy, 109-110, 112, 114

Manipulation, 100-101
Marital relationships, 14-15, 17, 25-28,
   99-100
Marriage, successful, 31-32
Masking, 99, 100-103
Maslow, Abraham, 85-88
Mental health, 84
Mistakes, 118
Morale, 73, 75

Needs, human, 52, 86-89

Oedipus Complex, 40
Openness, 68, 85, 94

Pain 39, 94, 96, 106
Parenthood, 51
Parenting, 36-37, 50-52, 55-57, 106
Peak experiences, 88
Personal fulfillment, 87-88
Praise, 102, 112-113, 108
Problem-solving sessions, 25-27
Puzzle, jigsaw, 109-110

Responsibility, 39, 96, 125
Rogers, Carl, 36
Romance, 63

Security, 44, 86, 94
Self-blame, 92-94
Self-confidence, 94
Self-esteem, 9-10, 51, 72, 87, 94, 101
Self-interest, 83
Self-statement(s), 95-96
Self-worth, 37, 88
Semantics, 122
Sex, 18-20, 108
Shakespeare, William, 91, 127
Spanking, 107-108
Superego, 93
Survival, 86,